7 Mindsets for Success, Happiness and Fulfilment

Swami Mukundananda, an alumnus of IIT and IIM, is a world-renowned spiritual teacher. He has dedicated his life to guiding millions worldwide on the path of happiness and fulfilment. His unique and profound approach to self-improvement blends scientific theories and perfect logic with his decades-long mastery of Vedic scriptures. As an expert on mind management and yogic sciences, he teaches many powerful yet simple techniques for life transformation. He lectures seven days a week, conducting seminars, workshops and retreats all over the world, including at Fortune 500 corporations and Ivy League universities.

7 Mindsets for Success, Happiness and Fulfilment

SWAMI MUKUNDANANDA

First published by Westland Publications Private Limited in 2019

1st Floor, A Block, East Wing, Plot No. 40, SP Infocity, Dr MGR Salai, Perungudi, Kandanchavadi, Chennai 600096

Westland and the Westland logo are the trademarks of Westland Publications Private Limited, or its affiliates.

Copyright © Radha Govind Dham, 2019

ISBN: 9789388754392

Typeset by Jojy Philip, New Delhi - 110015

*This book is dedicated to Jagadguru Shree Kripalu-ji Maharaj,
who munificently taught me the perennial Vedic knowledge,
and inspired me to consecrate my life to the dissemination of
divine wisdom, for the benefit of humankind.*

CONTENTS

INTRODUCTION

The Importance of Mindsets

What is the essential ingredient for a successful life? What is the one thing that can bestow upon us professional excellence, good health, familial comfort and inner joy?

That one thing is not money, for we find so many wealthy people who are unproductive, unhealthy and miserable. It is not powerful connections either, because even children of well-connected people sometimes end up as irresponsible derelicts or wayward vagrants. Nor is it high IQ, for many intellectuals are both emotionally fragile and socially obtuse. All these assets and qualities can undoubtedly prove helpful for success, but without that one essential ingredient, it cannot be guaranteed.

The biggest key to accomplishment, happiness and fulfilment is mastery over our emotions. As the saying goes, 'Attitude leads to altitude.' Those who are expert in marshalling their sentiments are catapulted to success in their field of work, despite overwhelming odds. Since they possess the ability to choose their thoughts, they fill themselves with faith and inspiration and apply themselves to their tasks with joy. They are resilient and determined, even while facing enormous challenges. Thus, they rise head and shoulders above their brethren, with astonishing accomplishments and heroic qualities of head and heart. Some may say these people just got lucky, but it was really their superior attitude in all situations that made all the difference.

In contrast, there are people who keep getting entangled in the cobwebs of their thoughts. They waste precious time and energy revisiting sentiments of anxiety, gloom and resentment. Such negative feelings rob them of health, make them unpopular among friends and ineffective at work. Consequently, their own mind becomes their worst enemy. Often, they do not even realise that their gloomy thoughts are the primary cause of their frustrations. And when they do become aware of their flawed thinking, they do not know how to subdue the despair that keeps cropping up in their mind. They may claim that Lady Luck never shone upon them, but, in reality, it was their ineptness at managing their emotions that tripped them on the journey of life.

To improve our attitudes, we require:

1) Knowledge of the sentiments, emotions and feelings that help or harm us.
2) The ability to react positively to the circumstances in our life, the people we interact with and the work we do.
3) To make the desirable attitudes a second nature to us, so they arise subconsciously, without effort.

How to Develop a Mindset

The attitudes we harbour habitually within ourselves become our mindsets. They are our customary ways of thinking, which have become an integral part of our personality. They can be compared to physical habits we create by repeating physical behaviours again and again until they begin to happen automatically. Similarly, mindsets are mental habits we establish internally, by practising particular attitudes repeatedly, until they come naturally to us. These mindsets can either work in our favour by flooding our consciousness with positivity or against us by plunging our mind into negativity.

Fortunately for us, harmful mindsets can be replaced by productive ones, without any prerequisite for external situations or resources. All we need to do is to change the way we think and feel. **The beauty of the power of mindset is that it is an internal resource we all possess.** If we can train our mind and intellect, their immense potential will get unlocked. Then, because of our advantageous mindset, we will naturally think productively in every situation.

When we study the lives of successful personalities, we discover a commonality in their outstanding mindsets. Consider, for example, the inspiring story of Thomas Edison.

When Thomas Edison was a five-year-old, his teacher called his mother and said, 'Take your little Tommy away. He is too dull to study.' His mother responded, 'My little Tommy is not stupid. I will teach him.' After that, Thomas had no further schooling, and he was home-schooled by his mother. Later, as an impoverished youth, he earned a living by selling candy on trains. He had begun losing his hearing as a child due to scarlet fever. The problem was further exacerbated when a train conductor hit him on his ear, making him partially deaf.

Edison had once saved the life of a three-year-old child, whose father was so grateful that he helped Thomas become a telegraph operator. That was the turning point for Edison, and from there, he launched his career as an inventor. He went on to become the greatest inventor in American history. In his lifetime, he held 1,093 US patents in his name. More significant than the number of patents was the tremendous impact his inventions have had in improving the quality of life for the entire humankind.

It is said that while working on inventing the electric bulb, Thomas Edison constantly failed before succeeding in his four-thousandth attempt. After he had failed for the 3,999th time, a journalist asked him, 'Mr Edison, are you not disappointed that you have repeatedly failed in your efforts?'

He responded firmly, 'Young man, let me teach you a lesson that will help you all your life. I did not fail for the 3,999th time; I only eliminated the 3,999 ways the electric bulb cannot be made.'

Thomas Edison's mindset of positivity, optimism and hope stood him in good stead, and in his next attempt, he succeeded in developing the electric bulb, without which life would be unimaginable today.

Proper mindsets are thus the forte of successful people. They are masters of their emotions and know how to manage their moods in any situation. Stories of the positive mindsets of successful people are available for all, as examples. They can help others develop in themselves the correct attitudes, and yet, only a few utilise their immense potential. What comes in the way?

Awful Attitudes Are the Bane

In contrast to the successful are those whose life is in tatters. They too wish to be efficacious, but their own appalling emotions become stumbling blocks, and trip them up again and again. Either they do not realise the importance of improving their thinking, or they get so overwhelmed by the negativity their mind creates that positive thoughts elude them. Franklin Roosevelt, a legendary president of the US, described this pitiable state perfectly when he said, 'Men are not prisoners of fate, but only prisoners of their own minds.'

Similarly, Samuel Johnson, a famous British writer, pointed out the uncontrolled mind as the primary reason for failure. 'With an unquiet mind, neither exercise, nor diet, nor physic can be of much use.'

Some examples of poor attitudes are:

- **The disease of thinking in terms of 'I' or 'me'**: People affected by this disease are so full of themselves that they do not realise they are obnoxious to others.
- **Petty jealousy**: Those with this sentiment resent the success of others. They believe everyone deserves equal success, regardless of their abilities, output or interpersonal skills.
- **Failure to forgive**: Such people continue to harbour grudges against others who have inflicted harm upon

them. They do not realise that grudges hurt *them* more than they hurt anyone else.

- **Fault-finding nature:** Those with such an attitude are experts at seeing shortcomings even in the best of things. They have a long and inexhaustible list of complaints and remain ever dissatisfied, even with the noblest of endeavours.

These are only a few examples of the many kinds of poor attitudes that people harbour within the inner recesses of their mind. Unfortunately, such attitudes act as emotional brakes preventing accomplishment and spiritual unfoldment in life. Let us try to understand this concept with an example.

A man woke up from his sleep one beautiful morning and lurched out of bed, realising that he had overslept. He had an important appointment at his office that day. So he rushed through his daily ablutions, munched a hasty breakfast and hopped into his car.

Quickly turning on the engine, he pressed the accelerator, expecting the car to lunge forward. Instead, he found it crawling. In frustration, he increased the pressure on the pedal, but it was in vain. He smelt burning rubber and found fumes emerging from the hood. He got out and discovered that the rubber brakes were melting. The mistake now dawned upon him—he had forgotten to disengage the parking brake!

The experience of life is very similar. We push hard to reach our goals and when progress is not visible, we push even harder, without realising that we have our emotional brakes

6

on. These brakes are emotions like greed, discontentment, fear, anxiety, stress and resentment. With these mental brakes engaged, trying harder does not help us. In fact, it may backfire in the form of a physical breakdown or a mental wear out. The secret, then, is not to try harder but smarter, by disengaging the emotional brakes of harmful attitudes that reside within.

It is pertinent to note that we are not born with murky mindsets—they get created, consciously or unconsciously, by the repetition of dismal emotions. They can be altered by the repetition of noble sentiments and sublime thoughts. Thus, an attitude of success is as easy to create as an attitude of failure, but the payoffs are immensely different.

So far, we have discussed the material benefits of having the right mindsets. Let us now see their spiritual rewards.

The Right Mindset Unlocks Spiritual Treasures

The right attitudes not only help us in our material pursuits but they also bestow upon us the spiritual rewards of divine knowledge, divine bliss and divine love. Mastery of emotions is an essential prerequisite for progress on the journey to enlightenment. **The principle is simple—we learn to become better persons by learning to harbour better thoughts.**

This self-evident fact is often missed out in religious practices. People perform external rituals without cultivating devotional sentiments. They physically travel to holy places but keep their worldliness inside. They decorate the deities they worship with their hands but forget to adorn their emotions. They bathe their physical bodies in sacred rivers but neglect to cleanse the impure thoughts hiding within. They offer clarified butter into sacrificial fires but ignore the oblation of their ego to God.

All the Vedic scriptures teach us that spirituality is a journey within ourselves. It entails the unfoldment of the inherent divinity inside us, which requires purification of the mind. External rituals are useful only as far as they help us make our thoughts sublime. But without cultivating beautiful and noble sentiments, empty ceremonies serve no purpose. The *Pañchadaśhī* states:

mana eva manuṣhyāṇāṁ kāraṇaṁ bandha mokṣhayoḥ

'Both bondage and liberation depend upon the state of our mind.' The Shreemad Bhagavatam states:

chetaḥ khalvasya bandhāya muktaye chātmano matam
guṇeśhu saktaṁ bandhāya rataṁ vā puṁsi muktaye

(3.25.15)

'Bondage and liberation are determined by the mind. Attachment of the mind in the realm of the three *guṇas* results in bondage, while detachment from material objects leads to release from maya (God's material energy).' Jagadguru Kripalu-ji Maharaj, the fifth original Jagadguru of the world, states:

bandhana aura mokṣha kā kāraṇa manahi bakhāna
yāte kauniu bhakti karu karu mana te hari dhyāna
(*Bhakti Śhatak*, verse 19)

'The mind is responsible for both bondage of maya and liberation from it. Hence, whatever form of devotion you practise, do not forget to remember God alongside.'

We have seen how learning to instal divine mindsets in our psyche is one of the most beneficial pursuits we can undertake in life. It confers upon us accomplishment, happiness and fulfilment. As we go through the book, we will discuss this sublime art in detail. But before we proceed in that direction, let us understand what provides us with the ability to choose our mindsets.

Objective vs Subjective Reality

We all have our unique ways of perceiving the world around us. Some see it as a dangerous place. Others feel that it is imbued with love. Some find the world predominantly evil, while others see the face of God in all people and things. Why is it that the same creation is viewed so differently by all?

The reason for this disparity is that there are two realities. **The external world around us is the objective reality.** It is the same for everyone—the way God has created it. However, our perception of this external world is a choice we make. It establishes our subjective reality—how we perceive the world. Since we all view the world differently, our personal realities are also different.

For example, if we are cheated by three attorneys in succession, we may conclude that all attorneys are cheats, without realising that this is only our perspective and not an objective truth.

Similarly, some people maintain a gloomy attitude towards life. The way they choose to see the circumstances in their life may be different from the way they actually are. The problem is that **when people harbour negativity in any situation, they forget that it is just their subjective perspective.** Others in the same situation may still choose to be cheerful and positive.

The example below will illustrate the difference in the mindsets of two people. They lived in the same room, and thus, their objective reality was identical. Yet, they harboured such contrasting attitudes that their subjective realities were poles apart.

Two critically ill patients, Santosh and Chanchal, were on adjacent beds of a double-bed hospital room. A close bond developed between them as they shared stories about their childhood, school days, professions, wives, children, dreams, successes, failures, and so on.

Both were bedridden, but for one hour every day, the nurses would make Santosh sit up, to drain out fluid from his lungs. Since his bed was next to the only window in the room, he would get to look out during that one hour and would describe what he saw to Chanchal.

Outside, there was an idyllic garden with quaint trees and benches in tranquil locations. All types of interesting people could be seen reclining on the benches. In the centre of the garden was a pond adorned with a beautiful fountain. Attracted by its cool waters, migratory birds would visit it for a bath. There were also flower beds with beautiful roses, tulips, daisies and daffodils in full blossom.

On hearing Santosh's description of the garden, Chanchal's world would brighten up. The world outside was so divinely sublime, in contrast to the dreary hospital ward with its smell of tinctures and medicines. Chanchal began to wait for the one hour when Santosh would be made to sit up, for he would get to hear about the latest addition to the scenic beauty of the garden.

One day, an evil thought entered Chanchal's mind. 'Why does my friend alone get to see the loveliness of the outside world while I rot in my bed? Why is God benevolent towards him alone?' Chanchal should not have thought like that, but he did. He allowed negative feelings to take root in his mind, and before he knew it, they had created more negativity until his mind became a cesspool of emotional hurt and resentment. 'I detest him,' he thought. 'He has all the fun. How unfair!'

Chanchal's mental state deteriorated until he could not stand the company of his roommate. One night, Santosh began coughing. Although he coughed often, this time it was very intense. He was breathing with great difficulty and seemed to be choking. In desperation, he clutched his pillow and bedsheet, but the cough showed no sign of respite. The obvious thing to do in such a situation would have been for Santosh to press the emergency bell. However, in his unbearable discomfort, the thought did not come to him.

The next best thing would clearly have been for Chanchal to press his emergency bell. But Chanchal was seething with such bitterness that he thought, 'He is suffering. Good! He deserves it. I loathe him.'

Santosh continued to cough for a few more painful minutes until all was quiet. The silence of the night descended upon the room. Next morning, the hospital attendants discovered the dead body and removed it without much ado.

Chanchal waited for a couple of days, to prevent any suspicion falling on him, and then made a request. 'Can my bed be moved to the other side, by the window?' he asked.

'Fair enough,' said the attendants. They moved him to the window side.

The next morning, Chanchal made another request. 'I am now sufficiently well. Can I sit up for a while?'

'That is a reasonable demand,' said the nurse on duty. She raised him to a sitting position.

Chanchal was excited. Finally, he was going to view the magnificent garden that Santosh used to enjoy describing. However, when he peered out, he was shocked. All he could see was the stark wall of a neighbouring building. 'What is this?' he mumbled.

The nurse answered, 'Adjacent to the hospital is a large warehouse. Since it is close, it blocks the entire view from the window.'

'Then what was it that my ex-roommate used to describe to me?' enquired a bewildered Chanchal.

'That was the beauty of his mind,' the nurse responded.

What Santosh had chosen to see was not the reality of the world outside his hospital window, but the loveliness of his mind within. His inner world was so beautiful that it refused to be subjugated by the dreary environment of the infirmary. Instead, he had preferred to think of beauty, serenity, harmony and love. As the saying goes:

Two men looked out from the prison bars
One saw the mud; the other saw the stars.

The point to note is that we all have the freedom to view our environment, relatives and work as we wish. But the way we utilise this choice has its consequences. When we repeatedly bring certain types of feelings to our mind, they develop into an attitude. And that attitude, when it hardens and becomes natural to our personality, develops into a mindset.

The Problem Is Not With the World, but With Our Mindset

When we are harassed or frustrated, it is natural to hold the circumstances around us responsible for the situation we are in. However, as surprising as it may seem, there is no flaw in the world that exists around us. It is created by God, who is perfect, all-knowing and infinitely merciful. Therefore, the world He has created is also perfectly made for the elevation of our soul. The Vedas state:

puruṣha evedaṁ sarvaṁ yadbhūtaṁ yachcha bhavyam
(*Śhwetāśhvatar Upaniṣhad* 3.15)

'All that existed in the past, all that is presently existing, and all that will exist in future, is the veritable form of the Lord.'

vāsudevaḥ sarvamiti   (Bhagavad Gita 7.19)

'The Supreme Lord Shree Krishna is everywhere in the world.'

Accordingly, elevated souls who purify their attitudes and ennoble their sentiments perceive the presence of God in every

13

atom of creation. The gopis of Vrindavan, who were considered the most exalted devotees of Lord Krishna, sang:

vāṭana meṅ, ghāṭana meṅ, vīthina meṅ, bāgana meṅ
belina meṅ, vāṭikā meṅ, phūlana meṅ, vana meṅ
darana meṅ, dīvārana meṅ, deharī darīchana meṅ
hīrana meṅ, hārana meṅ, bhūṣhaṇa meṅ, tana meṅ
kānana meṅ, kuñjana meṅ, gopana meṅ, gāyana meṅ
gokula meṅ, godhana meṅ, dāminī meṅ, ghana meṅ
jahañ jahañ dekhūñ tahañ śhyām hī dikhāyī deta
mero śhyām chhāya rahyo nainana meṅ tana meṅ

'Wherever I look, I see the enchanting form of my Beloved Shree Krishna. I see Him in all the paths, hills, lanes and parks. He is in the vines, the gardens, the flowers and the forests. The doors, the walls, the furniture and the windows are all imbued with His presence. He resides in the necklaces, garlands, ornaments and on my body itself. I see Shree Krishna's divine form in the jungle, the tree groves, the cowherd boys and the cows as well. He makes His divine presence felt in the divine land of Gokul, in the cows, in the flash of lightning, and in the clouds. Wherever I look, I see Shyamsundar. My Lord dwells in my eyes and mind.'

In this way, saints with purified attitudes see God everywhere in creation. Such a divine vision is not a figment of their imagination. Factually, God is all-pervading. The omnipresent Lord merely becomes evident to the saints who have cleansed their mind.

We, too, live in the same world as the saints. Why, then, do we find ourselves being attacked by foul moods and odious emotions? Though we may blame people or circumstances for it, the real problem is our sour attitude. All it takes to dispel gloom is to replace wretched thoughts with awesome ones. The story below will illustrate this:

A man once came to me in deep despair, as if his world had been shattered. He had been a member of our satsang in Cuttack, Odisha, India, for the last six years, and I was concerned for him. 'What is the matter with you?' I asked him.

'Swami-ji, you have no idea what a terrible thing has happened to me. My in-laws have come to live with me for two years, and it is creating hell for me. I cannot ask them to go because that will annoy my wife immensely. I love her, but I can never learn to get along with my in-laws. Their unwanted presence at home has made me so melancholic that I am scared I may slip into depression.'

The man implored me for a solution to his woes.

I asked him, 'Do you have dogs at home?'

'No,' he responded.

'Then the solution is quite simple,' I said. 'Take a litter of puppies to your home.'

The man obeyed. He promptly went to the market and bought four puppies. After five days, he came to me again.

I asked him, 'How is your mind now? Have the puppies helped in calming your nerves?'

'Unfortunately, my nerves have become even more jumpy,' he exclaimed. 'The puppies run all over the place, spreading confusion and disorder.'

I said, 'Never mind. Do you have any cats in your home?'

'No,' he replied.

'Then I have the perfect remedy for you,' I said. 'Bring two cats—one white and one black—and keep them in your backyard.'

Again, the devotee abided by my guidance. However, he returned three days later. 'Is your problem solved?' I asked.

'Swami-ji, it has exacerbated. The puppies cannot tolerate the cats and do not miss an opportunity to chase them around the backyard. I have to watch them all the time so that they remain inside the house.'

'Do not worry,' I said. 'Do you have cows?'

'No,' he responded.

I then told him, 'That is the whole problem; I have diagnosed it now. Bring a cow and its calf. Take good care of them and utilise the milk from the cow to feed your family and pets.'

The man appeared worried about the solution I had pushed onto him. Nevertheless, he returned home and did as advised. After a few days he came back to me, bristling with exasperation.

'What kind of Swami-ji are you?' he exclaimed. 'I came to you with the problem of my in-laws living with me, and you compounded it with a whole farmhouse of animals.'

'Never mind,' I said. 'You are only a step away from the solution. Now get rid of all the animals.'

The man hurriedly sold or gave away all the pets he had acquired. He returned to me after four days.

'Are you happy now?' I asked him.

'Yes, Swami-ji. I have found great peace in my home.'

The man's in-laws were still at home—it was the same situation in which he had felt disturbed earlier. But now he was relieved and incomparably more peaceful than before. All that was required was a change in his attitude.

The moral of the story is that external situations are often not in our control. Undesirable things happen and unwelcome people or circumstances come into our lives. The choice we have is to either feel miserable about what we cannot change or adjust what we can, which is our attitude.

It is said that life is 10 per cent what happens to us and 90 per cent how we react to it. Hence, we are about as happy as we decide to be. In other words, we do not need to go on a vacation or possess one crore rupees to be happy. In fact, if we have sufficient control over our mind, we need no other prerequisite for happiness.

When I first went to the US, I noticed a restaurant in many cities, named 'TGIF'. I wondered what kind of a name that was. When I asked someone, I was informed, 'Swami-ji, TGIF means "Thank God It's Friday". People are distressed from Monday to Friday because they have to work. So, on Friday evening, they think of the weekend ahead and feel happy.'

But that kind of a thought process has a downside to it. If we can only be happy on weekends, it means that we will be unhappy on weekdays. So four-and-a-half days will pass in misery, in anticipation of the two-and-a-half days of joy.

However, with the proper mindset, we do not need to wait for Friday to be happy. We can choose to think happy thoughts every day of the week and say, 'Thank God it's Monday!' or 'Thank God it's Thursday!' Therefore, we must learn the art of being happy, no matter what day of the week and what time of the day.

We must also unlearn the art of manufacturing unhappiness. Let me share a story to illustrate what I mean by creating misery:

Once, while flying from Dubai to Delhi, I was sitting next to an Indian couple. The man was cheerful and pleasant, while his wife kept complaining about everything. The tea was too cold for her, the soft drinks were not cold enough, the seat was dirty and so on. Striking up a conversation with the gentleman, I came to know that he owned an IT company with offices in the US and India. He added, 'My wife is in the manufacturing business.'

That seemed very odd to me, as she looked like a simple housewife.

I asked, curious, 'What does she manufacture?'

The husband responded, 'She manufactures unhappiness. She is unhappy wherever she goes!'

That was so well put. We need to get out of the business of creating gloom. If that has been our profession, we must cheer up and transform ourselves into happy individuals. On a lighter vein, to tickle your rib, let me share a joke about manufacturing unhappiness:

Kaka Hathrasi, the famous Hindi humourous poet, was crying.

'Kaka, why are you crying?' asked a man.

'My uncle passed away and left me a fortune of one crore rupees,' said Kaka.

'Really!' the man responded. 'What is there to cry about it?'

'My second uncle passed away and left me a fortune of two crore rupees,' said Kaka.

'So? I do not understand why you are crying,' replied the man.

'My third uncle also passed away,' added Kaka. 'In his will, he bequeathed four crore rupees to me.'

'That is all the more reason you should not be crying!' exclaimed the man.

'No! I am very unhappy,' replied Kaka. 'I do not have any more uncles who will pass away and leave fortunes for me.'

This is definitely a case of manufacturing unhappiness. There was nothing in the circumstances of Kaka Hathrasi requiring him to be unhappy. His misery was simply a consequence of the mood he chose to harbour. His mind had manufactured the misery he was experiencing.

Let us not allow our thoughts to rob us of peace and joy, which are ours to claim through mastery of our mindsets. Rather, let us master our emotions through the techniques in this book, and then we will discover a million reasons to be happy.

The world is full of people who complain about their situations. They consider it their topmost and only priority to improve their external circumstances. If, instead, they applied even a fraction of this effort to improve their own emotions, they would find happiness knocking on their doors. As the saying goes, 'Pain is inevitable; misery is an option.' Nobody can force us to be miserable if we choose to be happy.

In this book, you will find the seven most important attitudes for success, happiness and inner growth. Before we discuss them, I would like to address a question that may arise in your mind at this point: 'Why seven mindsets—why not more or less?'

The Reason for Seven Mindsets

In 1956, George Miller, a cognitive psychologist from Princeton University, wrote one of the most highly cited papers in psychology. It was titled *The Magical Number Seven, Plus or Minus Two: Some Limits on Our Capacity for Processing Information* and was published in the journal *Psychological Review*.

Miller discovered that when people are given pieces of information, each piece containing two to three bits of data, their brain processes them well, up to a limit of seven pieces. After that, the brain's performance in processing and comprehending information declines.

As a result of his research, Miller also found that when people are presented with a list of names, letters or words, and then asked to repeat them, they can do so for seven items. When the list expands beyond seven, they begin to forget. Thus, the average short-term memory of young adults is seven items. It could vary, with one or two items more or less, but the average is seven. This is why phone numbers in the US began as a set of seven digits.

This memory span invariably remains the same across categories, despite changes in the nature of items in the lists. Miller thus concluded that memory span is not limited in terms of bits of information, but rather in terms of chunks. The brain uses chunking as a method for keeping groups of information accessible for easy recall.

Miller's research findings have now become famous as 'Miller's Law'. It states that the short-term working memory of an average person is limited to seven items.

Accordingly, I have chosen seven mindsets so that you may easily remember and implement them in your life. Coincidentally, these seven mindsets cover the entire sequence of steps necessary for achieving success, happiness and fulfilment in life. Let us now proceed to learn what they are and how we can develop them.

CHAPTER 1

THE MINDSET OF POSITIVE THINKING

Positive thinking is the mental nature of harbouring happy thoughts and an optimistic attitude. Positive thinkers are always cheerful and confident about life. They prefer to see the same glass as half-full, which the pessimists find half-empty. Rather than brooding over problems, they remain focussed on what they want, and how to get it. This makes them effective at work and joyous in their relationships.

Positive thinkers do not seek preconditions for a happy attitude. They do not wait for all the lights in their lives to turn green for being optimistic and cheerful. They are masters in the art of staying elated even when life challenges them with sufficient reasons to make them feel miserable. They know that the world is full of dualities, and negatives can never be eliminated from it. The Ramayan states:

jaṛa chetana guṇa doṣhamaya, viśhva kīnha karatāra
santa hansa guṇa gahahiṅ paya, parihari vāri vikāra

'The Creator has filled the world with opposites. We see both living beings and inanimate objects here, each endowed with virtues and defects. However, saintly persons know how to grasp the good and leave out the bad. They are much like the swans who, when served a mixture of milk and water, drink the milk and leave the water behind.'

Thus, positive thinking is a saintly virtue. The story below illustrates its power:

Dr Prasad was an old man whose wife had recently passed away. His children were well-settled abroad and busy with their lives. Therefore, not wanting to be a burden on his children, Dr Prasad decided to spend the rest of his years in an old-age home. He finalised the contract with the manager of the old-age home, who then instructed a nurse to show him his room.

While walking him to his room, the nurse began praising it lavishly. 'It has a very luxurious carpet,' she said.

'I like it!' replied Dr Prasad.

'There is a fireplace made from attractive red bricks,' said the nurse.

'Oh, how nice!' he responded.

'Beautiful landscape pictures decorate the walls of the room,' the nurse continued.

'I love them so much!' said Dr Prasad.

'But you have not even seen your room yet,' remarked the nurse with surprise. 'How can you love it without looking at it?'

Dr Prasad replied, 'I do not need to see it. Whether I like it or not doesn't depend upon the state of the room; it depends upon me.'

In the above story, Dr Prasad chose a happy attitude, irrespective of the room's actual condition. This is an example of positive thinking. When we habitually practise such positive emotions, they become an integral part of our nature. A positive attitude helps us in at least three significant ways:

1) It makes us a happier person
2) It improves our performance at work
3) It enhances our physical health

Let us take a look at each of these in further detail.

Positivity Makes Us Happier People

Ultimately, we all want to be happy, and it is for this singular objective that we do everything in life. Nobody pursues misery as their goal in life. If there are people who want suffering instead of happiness, they must be experts in hiding, because they are not visible anywhere.

Sometimes it may seem that people are deliberately courting misery. But it is only because they believe that after bearing with temporary distress, they will be able to enjoy long-term happiness. For example, a woman does not like physical exercise and yet follows a strict regimen of working out daily. She is only bearing the oppression of a daily workout because she has faith it will improve her health, and this, in turn, will give her joy. Thus, to say that some people want to be miserable is an incorrect statement. The universal common desire of humankind is the yearning to be happy, contented and joyous.

What does mindset have to do with our experience of joy? We invariably assume that happiness is a function of our material possessions. We believe that if we could own a Porsche, live in a five-bedroom home or be the CEO of a multinational corporation, we would surely be blissful. We believe external circumstances and objects will give us pleasure. But if we open our eyes and look around, we find the opposite to be true. Unfortunately, we cannot read the thoughts of those who possess material wealth, and so it seems to us that they are enjoying life. But if we could just peep into their minds, we would exclaim, 'My ... my ... such misery! I am happier than them.'

The testimony of John D. Rockefeller, the wealthiest American in modern history, revealed this pitiable state on his deathbed. He admitted, 'I have made many millions, but they have brought me no happiness.' The fact is that if you are not content when you possess a little, you will not be content even when you possess a lot. And if you do not share when you have a little, you will also not share when you have plenty. You might have read the story 'King Midas and the Golden Touch' in your childhood.

King Midas had no dearth of gold, but his greed knew no bounds. A fairy manifested before him and said, 'Ask for a boon.'

Midas responded, 'Anything I touch should turn into gold.'

The fairy bestowed the golden touch upon him. But he soon came to regret it, because when he tried to eat, his plate and all the food on it would turn to gold. When he tried to drink, the cup and the water in it would become gold. Soon, his beloved daughter came to him complaining, and when he reached out to console her with his touch, she turned into a golden statue. In despair, he called the fairy back and begged her to take away the horrible golden boon.

'Do you still think that gold is the greatest thing in the world?' asked the fairy.

'No! No!' responded King Midas. 'I have learnt my lesson. Now I do not want gold; I want peace and happiness.'

This old children's tale has continued to reverberate through the ages. The consulting rooms of psychiatrists are ever-busy with rich and famous patients, who came to the harsh realisation that a posh house, a beautiful spouse, expensive cars and societal accolades are not enough for peace and happiness. Yet, others continue the mad rush without pondering, 'Why is it that those ahead of me in the race are not happy?'

I came across a poem by Virginia Braiser titled 'Time of the Mad Atom', first published in 1949, that suitably depicts the crazy haste for material objects in these modern times:

This is the age of the half-read page.
The quick hash and the mad dash.
The bright night with the nerves tight.
The plane hop with the brief stop.
The lamp tan in a short span.
The Big Shot in a good spot.
And the brain strain and the heart pain.

And the cat naps till the spring snaps—
And the fun's done!

Unfortunately, happiness cannot be purchased at a five-star mall, nor is it a gift that the postman can deliver to our mailbox. The poet Rudyard Kipling once said:

Do not pay too much attention to fame, power or money. Some day you will meet a person who cares for none of these, and then you'll know how poor you are.

The elusive key to happiness lies not on the outside but within us. It can be accessed by developing a proper attitude. Let us understand this axiom from the following story:

In medieval times, there lived a king in a small nation. One evening, he was strolling on the terrace of his palace when he heard sounds of mirth and laughter from the hut adjacent to the wall of his castle. A poor family lived there. Despite their penury, they were enjoying each other's company, laughing and celebrating.

The king was astonished. He thought, 'How is this impoverished family having such a good time, while I, the king of the land, am unhappy?'

The king called his wise minister and asked him, 'Can you please teach me the secret of this poor family's happiness?'

The minister responded, 'O king, you have asked me for a rare and priceless gem of wisdom. I will reveal the secret to you, but I need ninety-nine gold coins for it.'

The king thought it was a small price for learning the art of happiness. He instructed his servants to bring the gold coins and hand them to the minister. The minister tied the ninety-nine pieces of yellow metal in a piece of cloth and threw the bundle in front of the poor family's hut.

In the morning, when the family woke up, they found the bundle at their doorstep. At first, they were apprehensive about what could be inside it. However, they mustered courage and, on untying it, discovered the gold coins.

They were delighted. 'A bundle of gold! God is so merciful. We had seen gold earlier, but only through the windowpanes of jewellery shops. Never in our dreams had we thought of being the proud owners of gold ourselves. When it rains, it pours. Let us see how much God has given us.'

They began counting the gold coins and discovered that there were ninety-nine. Now they were dissatisfied. 'If God had to give us gold, He should have given us a hundred coins. What sense was there in giving only ninety-nine?'

They decided to purchase the hundredth gold coin themselves, by saving up for it. To save a certain amount every day, they agreed upon a plan for increasing their earnings and decreasing their spendings. But when it would not happen, a fight would begin at home.

'You did not work hard enough,' the wife would tell the husband.

'It is not my fault,' the husband would respond. 'What was the need to cook in ghee?'

'You are the one who should have been more careful with the purchases,' the wife would retort. 'What was the need to buy a new kurta?'

Slowly, the peace in the house evaporated. A month later, the king was again strolling on the terrace of his palace when he heard sounds of quarrel emanating from the same hut. He was astounded at the drastic change. The king summoned his minister and asked, 'What happened to this family? They were blissful only a month ago, and now they seem to be miserable.'

The minister responded, 'O king, this is called the trap of ninety-nine. This family has fallen into the trap. The secret of their happy state earlier lay in being contented with what they had. But now, they are dissatisfied because they believe they own only ninety-nine gold coins, which is insufficient for their happiness. Therefore, they now need the hundredth gold coin to be happy.'

Let's ponder over the message conveyed by the above story. We may discover that it applies to us as well. Most of us reading this book have food to eat and clothes to wear—it is not that we are facing crushing poverty or dying of hunger—but our belief tells us, 'I cannot be happy yet, for what I have is only ninety-nine. I need a hundred to be blissful. Just one more ...'

In this way, we tie our happiness to a target that we strive towards, a set of objects we wish to own, or a position we hope to occupy. But these are all goals set for the future. In the meantime, life goes on while we wait anxiously for the future in order to be happy. And if we do finally achieve our cherished goal, there is still no guarantee it will satisfy us. Oscar Wilde, the famous Irish poet and playwright, expressed it very lucidly when he wrote:

There are only two tragedies in life: one is not getting what one wants, and the other is getting it.

Thus, the art of joyous living lies not in waiting to reach happiness in the future but in adjusting our attitude to discover it here and now. By developing a positive mindset, we can be happy, irrespective of external factors.

We have seen how the right attitude is the key to happiness. Let us now see how it helps us in our professional life.

Excellence at Work

Our performance at work does not depend as much on our skillset as it does upon our mindset. Very often, toppers from leading MBA programmes turn out to be ineffective in corporate life due to poor attitudes, despite being equipped with adequate theoretical knowledge of managerial techniques. On the other hand, by artful control over their emotions, students who had been at the bottom of their class move up the corporate ladder to become CEOs. This is the reason why, according to the *Companies Report on American Business*, 1983, 94 per cent of executives of Fortune 500 companies attribute their success to attitude more than any other personality trait.

While the right attitude helps us rise in our professional career, the opposite is also true. A poor mindset is often the biggest factor responsible for the sabotaging of one's career. A San Francisco consulting company, Robert Half International, surveyed one hundred of the largest firms in the US. They asked the senior executives of these companies to name the single most significant reason for firing their last three employees.

The results of the questionnaire revealed that only 17 per cent of the dismissals were for incompetence, while 83 per cent were related to attitude problems, such as dishonesty, lack of motivation and disobedience. Let us look into a few more studies and research corroborating this fact.

A double-blind test was done to study the correlation between the attitude of teachers and the performance of students. The research was conducted in San Francisco in the late 1960s by Dr Robert Rosenthal of Harvard University, who later described it in his book, *Pygmalion in the Classroom: Teacher Expectation and Pupils' Intellectual Development.*

At the beginning of the school year, three teachers were chosen randomly and called to the principal's office. The principal informed them, 'We have been observing your teaching style and have identified you as exceptional teachers on a secret performance scale. As a special reward for your teaching excellence, we are assigning you to high-performing students.' The teachers were overjoyed, for the dream of any teacher is the opportunity to have a classroom full of gifted students.

The students were similarly picked randomly, but they were told, 'Based on a secret criterion, we have identified you as the brightest students, with exceptional potential. Hence, we are assigning you to the best teachers.'

The group was monitored for a full year. It was observed that the teachers seemed to teach with greater commitment. They were more patient when students did not comprehend the lessons right away. They spent more time tutoring students after school. In case a child had difficulty grasping something, the teachers assumed that the problem was not in the student, but in their teaching.

At the end of the academic year, the three classes were not just the best in school but in the entire school district. Their grades improved by 20–30 per cent, in comparison to the previous year.

When the teachers learnt this, they responded, 'It is natural that our students' performance should be above average. After all, they are exceptional.'

Upon being informed that the students had been selected randomly, the teachers reasoned, 'In that case, we teachers must have done well, because we are the best in the school.' The teachers were then told that they had also been selected arbitrarily.

What caused the spectacular improvement in the performance of the group of randomly selected students? It was the positive mindset. Both the students and the teachers felt something remarkable was happening in their class. Such an attitude brought out the best in them.

The above observation is akin to the famous Hawthorne Effect in industrial engineering.

Between 1924 and 1932, experiments were conducted at the Western Electric plant in Cicero, Illinois, to study the possibility of improving the productivity of workers by adjusting the assembly line conditions. At first, the managers increased the illumination level in the factory. Production increased. Later, the illumination was decreased in a controlled manner. Again, it improved production. Management was astonished. They tried various permutations: giving two five-minute breaks, one ten-minute break, allowing people to select coworkers, assigning compatible coworkers, etc. To the amazement of the researchers, each change led to an increase in output, even if the modification was the reverse of what had been done previously.

These results were then interpreted by Elton Mayo, an organisational psychologist, who hypothesised that the changes were not the cause for enhanced productivity. Rather, the environmental adjustments led the workers to believe that they were being cared for. This boosted their morale and led to improved performance. The phenomenon is now well known as the 'Hawthorne Effect'.

All the above examples highlight how a positive mindset improves work performance. Let us now see how attitude affects our physical health.

Connection between Emotions and Health

The amalgamation of body and mind works miraculously. If the number of processes taking place within were to be replicated by machines, it would require a medium-sized factory, and the sound generated from it would be audible half a mile away. But all that complex mechanism is packed within our six-foot frame, and the processes inside us happen so silently that doctors need stethoscopes to hear them!

Even more miraculous than the amazing body is the subtle machine that is the mind. The *Yog Vāsiṣṭh* states:

kṣhaṇamāyāti pātālaṁ kṣhaṇaṁ yāti nabhasthalam

'The mind is so nimble that in a moment it travels down to the nether regions, and in the next moment, it is up in the celestial skies.'

One of the functions of the mind is to generate thoughts. These thoughts have the power to raise our blood pressure or lower it, to increase our heartbeat or drop it, to make us happy or sad, and to change the chemical composition of our blood. Thus, we can become healthy or unwell by the thoughts we harbour.

Half a century ago, if someone claimed that negative thoughts caused a physical affliction, the medical profession would reject the idea as heresy. But over the last four decades, greater awareness about the correlation between our emotional state and physical health has evolved.

Let us look at this mind-body connection a little closely. You may have heard of Pavlov's experiments, wherein he gave food to dogs, and at the same time, rang a bell. On seeing the food, the dogs would begin salivating. After a few days, Pavlov found that even when no food was brought, the ringing of the bell alone would cause the dogs to salivate. The dogs had begun associating the sound of the bell with the serving of food. The mental stimulus would produce the physical response of salivation in the dog. This is one of the simplest cases of mind-body response.

In recent times, various studies have been conducted to understand the impact of the mental state of human beings on their bodies. One such study was in the dental field.

In most cases, when the lower wisdom teeth are extracted, the gums swell up post-surgery. To control the swelling, dentists prescribe massaging with a dental instrument attached to an ultrasound machine. As a result, the swelling disappears in 30 per cent of the cases.

A few decades ago, researchers at King's College, London, conducted an experiment. They used an ultrasound machine with zero frequency waves on patients. It appeared to be working, but actually, it was not emitting any rays.

At first, it was placed at one particular spot on the patients' swollen gums. The swelling reduced for 35 per cent of the patients. Next, the instrument with zero emissions was moved around on the patients' jaws. The swelling was found to reduce in 30 per cent of the cases.

Finally, the machine was given to the patients. They were told to hold it on their jaw themselves. This time, the swelling reduced for only 15 per cent of the patients, but it still worked. The results revealed that the mere thought of being cured was sufficient for effecting the healing in a patient.

The above findings are similar to the placebo effect, which is the psychological healing that takes place through dummy pills. In this procedure, when a patient visits a physician complaining of sickness, the doctor says, 'I am giving you the best possible drug for your ailment.' But, instead, a dummy pill is administered, and by consuming it, the patient's condition improves. The cure cannot be attributed to the contents of the medicine, which, obviously, has no curative powers. It is the patient's belief that effects the cure.

The placebo effect is sometimes considered a demeaning term. If you tell someone, 'You were cured by a placebo' that person feels slighted, 'You mean my sickness was only a creation of my mind?' Therefore, a better term for the placebo effect is 'remembered wellness'. It is the phenomenon of subconsciously remembering the state of wellness and replicating it to improve our health.

The medical profession is well aware of this phenomenon. For example, a patient is experiencing acute symptoms of a viral throat infection. He or she visits a physician for consultation. The doctor says, 'Let me take a look,' and peers into the patient's mouth. On examining the throat, the doctor pronounces, 'You are perfectly fine.' The patient is astonished to know that the symptoms have disappeared. How did the cure take place?

The patients' visit to the doctor reassured their subconscious mind, 'I will get well.' It resulted in 'remembered wellness' and the body healed itself. This connection of the biological response to the state of mind has significant consequences for the medical profession. It is a documented fact that when a doctor reassures the patient with caring words, it increases the efficacy of the prescription.

Jagadguru Shree Kripalu-ji Maharaj often emphasised the impact of good behaviour by relating the story of his schoolmate. This person had opted for a career in medicine. Although he was not an accomplished doctor, his patients would still get cured because of the loving care with which he tended to them.

Thus, 'remembered wellness' is a medically confirmed phenomenon. The other side of it is 'remembered illness', when your mind remembers a sickly condition and the body replicates it to become ill. A common example is 'white collar hypertension'. Many patients have perfect blood pressure at home, but when they visit the doctor, they find their blood pressure has increased. The reason is that their mind thinks, 'I am in a clinic and am surrounded by patients, so I must be unwell.' Such thoughts raise blood pressure. This is a case of 'remembered illness'; of the mind making the body sick.

An extreme example of 'remembered illness' was given by Dr Herbert Benson, professor of mind/body medicine at Harvard Medical School. In his book, *The Relaxation Response*, Dr Benson has described the behaviours of the Aboriginal tribes of Australia.

They have a primitive custom of the witch-doctor boning people he dislikes. These simple-minded tribal people believe that if their witch-doctor incants certain spells and bones them, there is no way they can continue to live. Dr Benson describes the scene that takes place.

When the witch-doctor gets annoyed and waves a bone before someone, while chanting and lifting his other hand skyward, that unfortunate person's expression changes completely. He thinks, 'Now I am done for; I am a goner; there is absolutely no hope.'

In a few minutes, that person is suffocating. A little while later, clasping his throat, he falls to the ground. As unfortunate and grotesque as it may seem, in a few hours, the person passes away.

This is a graphic illustration of the mind making the body sick. The reason for the failure of the physical bodily processes was that the non-physical intellect decided, 'I have no chance of survival; I just cannot live.'

The above is an extreme example leading to death. In milder instances, **the mind-body connection creates what are called 'psychosomatic illnesses'.** These are physical diseases having psychological causes. Various studies have revealed that psoriasis, eczema, stomach ulcers, high blood pressure and heart disease, all have a high correlation with the mind. Patients with these afflictions have experienced that at any given time, their current emotional state can affect the intensity of their disease.

One common emotional state that aggravates physical afflictions is stress. When we feel stressed, the hypothalamus in the brain signals the adrenal cortex to produce cortisol. It also cues the adrenal medulla to produce epinephrine. The release of these hormones causes the liver to produce more glucose. If that is not used up, it makes one susceptible to diabetes. Thus, the link between stress and diabetes is a confirmed medical fact.

Stress also increases blood pressure in the short term, and so, chronic stress contributes to permanently high blood pressure. Scientific studies have also established that when we are stressed out, the immune system gets suppressed, making us more vulnerable to bacterial infections and viruses.

Furthermore, people who harbour excessive stress over a long term have a higher risk of cardiovascular diseases. This risk is particularly higher in those who tend to be excessively competitive, impatient and hostile. Of these characteristics, hostility is said to be the most significant.

But the converse is also true. If our emotional state is positive and optimistic, our physical health gets boosted as well. Research has revealed that compassionate and kind thoughts towards others increases production of a hormone called serotonin in the brain. Serotonin makes us feel good, which, in turn, strengthens our immune system. Amazingly, others who see our acts of kindness also experience an increased production of serotonin. Consequently, kindness has the same effect as an antidepressant drug.

So far, we have explored the benefits of positive thinking in the following ways:

1) Experiencing happiness
2) Better performance at work
3) Improved physical health

With this inference, let us now create a desire to eradicate negative thoughts from our psyche. How do we proceed to do that?

The Art of Positive Thinking

What generates negative emotions in us? What prevents us from harbouring positive thoughts? What makes us rivet our mind on the deficiencies and shortfalls in our life? What blinds us from seeing the many blessings we have received?

It is the unforgiving ego, which is the principal enemy of spiritual thinking. It tells us that our desires are of paramount importance, for we are the centre of the universe. Our ego is under the illusion that the universe has been made for the fulfilment of our puny desires. It makes us behave like the geologist in the story below:

A geologist started on an expedition along the river Ganges. He was travelling on foot, exploring the river bank and verifying its course with a map. However, at one place, he found that according to his map the river should be turning left, while it was actually flowing right. He was greatly annoyed. 'How come the Ganges does not follow my map? It is pointless to explore it.' He dumped his map and returned home.

To expect the Ganges to adhere to the map was childish. Instead, it was the map that should have conformed to the river. But in his obstinacy, the geologist was expecting the world to conform to his puny conceptions.

Though the above example may seem absurd, our ego makes us behave in exactly the same manner. It deceives us into believing that the world exists for the fulfilment of our desires. We forget that God is the centre of the universe, not us, and the entire creation is for His sake. We are meant to fulfil the will of God and not the other way around.

This is why it is worthwhile to remember that EGO is an acronym for Edging God Out. The German philosopher, Paul Deussen, expressed this very nicely when he wrote:

Egotism is like a cloud that keeps God hidden from our sight. If, by the mercy of the true guru, egotism vanishes, then God is seen in His full glory.

When we efface our self-conceit, we then begin to appreciate the many graces we have received. We stop taking them for granted as we hitherto did. Previously, we may have made much ado about the few miseries on our plate, but when humility makes its home in our consciousness, we become aware of the numerous blessings we have received as the following story illustrates.

Abheer had a terrible itch in his eyes. He showed it to the doctor who diagnosed, 'You have a cancerous growth in your eyes. You will have to undergo surgery for the removal of your eyeballs. That is the only way you can prevent the tumour from spreading to the rest of your body.'

Abheer's spirit was shattered. On the appointed day, he went to the surgery room, thinking he would be blind when he would come out of there. However, when the doctor cut into his eyes, he discovered that the problem was a rare fungus growing on the retina. He cleaned it up and sewed the incision together. In a couple of hours, Abheer regained consciousness.

On opening his eyes after a few days, he discovered that he was still able to see. Now Abheer's attitude was transformed. He thought, 'I am so grateful to God for allowing me to retain my eyes. By His infinite grace, He has bestowed on me the power of vision to continue seeing His beautiful creation!'

Earlier, Abheer had taken his eyes for granted, but he now appreciated them as blessings of God. Similarly, we too tend to take our home, possessions and health for granted. If we can only learn to be thankful to the Lord for these graces, we will find ample reasons for positive thinking.

The problem is, when we have something, we forget it is a blessing. Only later, in its absence, do we realise the value of what we had. We can learn this lesson from the husband and wife in the story below:

A couple I knew lived in a two-bedroom house in Arlington, Texas. It was comfortable and adequate for the two of them. But they were discontented seeing their friends' palatial houses in nearby Coppell. Whenever they met me, they expressed nothing but frustration for their home.

Unfortunately, about that time, the husband lost his job, which made them forfeit their mortgage payments. Their bank, after warning them for a few consecutive months, was about to foreclose on them. This would have left them on the streets, for they had no other investments.

For two full months, the thought of losing their house dangled like the sword of Damocles over their head. On the very day when the property was going to slip out of their hands, the husband miraculously got a new job, and their home was saved.

Now they live in the same house but see it in a different light. They repeatedly thank God for giving them a roof over their head. What do you think changed? Not their external assets, but their perspective.

It is our pride that makes us blind to God's innumerable graces. It deludes us into believing that the fulfilment of our selfish desires is the primary purpose of creation. It gives us a reason to justify our frustration when things do not go our way.

If we can learn to be humble, we will appreciate that the satiation of our egotistical desires is not the purpose of the universe. Instead, the aim of our life is to fulfil the will of God. This simple enlightenment will awaken us to the innumerable graces that have come our way, and in them, we will discover millions of reasons to be happy. This is the art of positive thinking, which is the first mindset for success, happiness and fulfilment.

When we subdue our selfish desires, we wake up to a higher purpose that God has in store for us and realise that the universe is not hostile to life. Rather, it is generous and eager to bestow infinite blessings and opportunities for the soul to evolve and manifest its divine destiny.

However, self-improvement can only happen when we internalise the second mindset for success, which is the mindset of taking responsibility for our shortcomings and weaknesses. Let us discuss this next.

CHAPTER 2

THE MINDSET OF TAKING RESPONSIBILITY FOR OUR EMOTIONS

In the previous chapter, we discussed the importance of keeping happy thoughts and an optimistic attitude in the temple of our mind. But what if a situation or a person evokes negativity in us? What should we do and whom should we blame for the adverse sentiments arising in our psyche?

Consider the following scenario:

You have a vitally important client meeting on the other side of town, scheduled for one afternoon. Calculating the driving time required, you plan to start from your office after lunch. But just as you are getting ready to leave, your niece phones and drags you into a pointless conversation that costs you fifteen priceless minutes.

When you finally get into your car, you need the extra speed to make up for the lost time. However, drivers keep cutting you off. Finally, you reach the highway, expecting to pick up speed. To your dismay, you find the cars inching forward. 'Trust my luck,' you think. 'I am caught in a traffic jam.' When you finally reach the neck of the jam, you discover the trivial cause for it. There has been no accident at all. The only unusual sight is two cars parked by the roadside, with their passengers loitering nearby. Unfortunately, everyone who is driving by is turning to see what the party is about, and that caused the traffic jam. This annoys you even further.

Ultimately, when you reach your client, you are forty-five minutes late. He gives you a piece of his mind, but because your company policy is 'client is king', you are forced to bear his berating sermon silently, and that caps your awful mood for the day.

Now, whom would you blame for your negative emotions? Is the client, who scolded you, responsible for your bad mood? Or the drivers who caused the traffic jam? Or the cars that rudely cut you off? Or your niece for calling you at the wrong time?

Actually, none of them is responsible for your emotions. No matter how terrible anybody's behaviour towards us, there is no justification for harbouring odious thoughts. Our feelings are a choice we make. The responsibility to control our mind is our own. Whether we harbour pleasant or miserable sentiments, we are accountable for the way we think.

The Gap between Circumstances and Our Emotions

No matter what the external situation, we are free to choose our emotional response. Understanding this gap between the circumstances and feelings provides us with a lever to control our sentiments. It frees the mind from the shackles of the environment. Only when this happens can we begin our journey towards purification of the mind and spiritual elevation.

Those who do not realise this gap between stimulus (the circumstances) and response (our emotions) falsely believe that the steering wheel of their feelings lies in the hands of others. Thus, they repeatedly suffer emotional ups and downs based on others' behaviours. When troubled by negativity, they feel desperate, for they are unable to control the external factors. However, they fail to realise their God-given freedom to choose positive feelings, irrespective of situations.

A wonderful endorsement of this free will was given by a Holocaust survivor of the Second World War, Viktor Frankl. He presented his memoirs in the book *Man's Search for Meaning*.

Frankl, an Austrian Jew, was a practising neurologist and psychiatrist with a deep interest in psychology. His mastery over the subject can be gauged from the fact that he submitted papers on psychology to Sigmund Freud, which impressed the famous psychologist so much that he got them published.

Unfortunately, when Hitler went on a rampage against Jews in Europe, Viktor Frankl was rounded up along with his family, and thrown into Auschwitz prison, the worst of the Jewish concentration camps. It was notorious for its inhuman treatment of prisoners. There, he was separated from his wife and daughter and later came to know they had died. Describing the barbaric treatment in the camp, Frankl mentions that, at times, he would be forced to walk naked through the night, not knowing if he would be alive the next morning.

*However, through the indescribable tribulations, he discovered one freedom he possessed that nobody could snatch from him. It was the ability to choose his emotional attitude. He decided to be cheerful, no matter what. Often, he would be seen smiling and even laughing. When others asked him how he could be happy, he responded that he did not have control over the external situation, but he did have control over his mind, and he would not let others disturb it. **He realised that a person who has nothing left in the world can still experience bliss by harbouring the right thoughts.***

He became an inspiration to his fellow prisoners and the guards. He decided to live through the ordeal and announce his discovery to others. Later, when the Second World War ended, and he was released from incarceration, he returned to Vienna. There, he began practising his profession once again, forming a new school of psychology called 'Logotherapy', also known as 'Third Viennese School of Psychotherapy'. It is based upon the attitude we have towards unavoidable suffering, and how we can find meaning in it.

Frankl travelled throughout the world, speaking in 219 universities and receiving twenty-nine honorary doctorates. There are more than 150 books in fifteen languages published about him.

The key takeaway from this story is that undesirable things do happen. Life does not always serve us chocolates and cakes. It also sends lemons our way. But do lemons turn us sour, or do we make lemonade out of them? This is dependent upon our ability to manage our emotions. Frankl exhibited the ultimate freedom we humans possess—the freedom to choose our feelings, irrespective of the circumstances.

Immensely successful people in history also hit rough weather on their life's journey. Nonetheless, the rain did not drench their spirit; instead, they utilised the opportunity to create rainbows in their lives. For example, Soordas was blind from birth, Meerabai was a widow, Kabirdas was of unknown parentage and Narsi Mehta and Tulsidas were ridiculed by society. Likewise, Beethoven was almost deaf when he created his best compositions, Abraham Lincoln was raised in abject poverty, Franklin Roosevelt had infantile paralysis and Stephen Hawking was physically challenged most of his life.

If these brilliant luminaries who blazed the earth had brooded over the list of items that God did not bestow upon them, they would have died in bitterness. On the contrary, they took charge of their attitudes and made the best of what they had received. Consequently, they left their mark on the sands of time.

In contrast, the vast majority of people focus on negative circumstances that are beyond their control. Thus, they fail to take responsibility for what they can change, which is their emotions, beliefs and behaviour. They develop the unproductive habit of playing the blame game, and never feel they have any personal responsibility to improve their moods.

Such people feel negative emotions 'happen to them' because of the environment. They hold their parents responsible for their sour nature, which they are convinced was scripted by their upbringing. And if it is not their parents, they blame their grandparents for providing them with faulty genes. If the grandparents are also not at fault, they accuse their circumstances—the boss, spouse, neighbour or the polity. Since they feel no obligation for their emotions, they also perceive no onus to practise mastery over their mental state.

These are the unfortunate ones who have forsaken their responsibility to control their mind. The word responsibility itself implies the freedom to choose. It is made from the words: 'response' and 'ability', meaning the ability to choose one's emotions regardless of the circumstance.

Mature vs Immature Behaviour

The responsibility for our mind lies with us. By honouring it, we ascend the spiritual heights reached by great saints. By relinquishing it, we lose the golden chance in the human form to manifest the divinity within us.

The sign of immaturity is to point fingers at others for our mood. Such juvenile behaviour is acceptable in childhood; for children, it is understandable and condoned. But as we grow up, we are expected to become mature and live our life by our values, not by the whims of our moods. The pity is that even in adulthood, many refuse to mature and remain kids emotionally. If you ask them why they are miserable, they blame others. 'It is all because of so-and-so.'

The sign of emotional immaturity is abdicating accountability for our thoughts. Often, people come and tell me, 'Swami-ji, my devotional sentiments have disappeared. I do not have the same feelings towards God and guru any longer.'

'So, what is the remedy to this problem?' I ask them.

'I am waiting for the sentiments to come back,' they respond.

'When will your devotional sentiments return?'

'I do not know, Swami-ji. But whenever they return, you will see me more often at the temple.'

They miss the point that their devotion is their responsibility. Devotion means to create divine sentiments and not to wait for the next wave of devotional emotions to arise from within. Devotion is not an adjective but a verb that describes our effort to harbour noble and sublime thoughts.

In the worldly realm as well, you find emotionally immature people saying, 'My love for my spouse has dried up. I do not have the same feelings any longer.' However, to think like this is foolishness. Are they waiting for loving sentiments to come upon them? And what if the loving sentiments do not arise again of their own accord? Whom will they hold responsible for the waning of their love?

In contrast, the emotionally mature understand that love is a choice they make. To truly love someone means to reject any unloving sentiments that the mind may suggest. Love requires exerting our heart and creating loving feelings towards the object of our affection.

This ability to exercise our free will for choosing our attitude is the foundation of spiritual growth. In the Bhagavad Gita, Lord Krishna said to Arjun:

uddhared ātmanātmānaṁ nātmānam avasādayet
ātmaiva hyātmano bandhur ātmaiva ripur ātmanaḥ   (6.5)

'Uplift yourself by the power of your mind, and do not degrade yourself; for the controlled mind can be your best friend, while the unbridled mind will be your worst enemy.'

The mind becomes an enemy when we allow ourselves to be controlled by its whims. It becomes our friend when we subjugate it to our values, aspirations and goals.

Until we realise our God-given freedom to select our attitude, we can never grow spiritually. Where we are in life today is the accumulated consequence of how we exercised our free will in the innumerable past lives as well as in this life. Where we go from here will depend upon the choices we make today. So, it is up to us to wake up every morning and don the attitude we decide is best for us.

The Biggest Fault Line Is Our Fault-finding Nature

There are many people who spend a lifetime blaming others for the mess they find themselves in. They are like the politician who got elected to public office but misutilised it to embezzle government funds.

On being caught and brought before the judge, the politician pleaded not guilty. 'It's not my fault, your honour,' he said. 'It is the fault of the people who voted me into office. Without their votes, this crime would never have taken place.'

Some time ago, psychologists did a study on prison inmates to see whether they owned up to their crimes. They inquired of the prisoners why they were in jail, and received answers like:

- 'It is not my fault. My wife betrayed me.'
- 'My business partner backstabbed me.'
- 'I am innocent. They framed me.'
- 'I was poor and had no options.'

None of the prisoners admitted to breaking the law. The psychologists concluded jokingly that there had never been a bunch of more innocent people in the world! The prisoners' responses were, of course, an extreme example of forsaken accountability, but even the slightest semblance of this thought pattern needs to be carefully detected and weeded out of our psyche. Else, we will not strive to move away from harmful thoughts and continue to justify our negative thinking with stories and alibis that our mind constructs.

If we have developed the pernicious habit of blaming everyone and everything but ourselves, we need to relook our paradigm. We need to do some serious soul-searching and see if our faulty attitude is making everybody seem bad to us. This is like the patient who complained of pain all over his body.

A patient once complained to the physician, 'Doctor, I am in terrible pain.'

'Where does it pain? Let me see,' the doctor said. He caught the patient's index finger and placed it on his forehead. 'Is it paining here?'

'Oh ... oh ... oh ... it is paining immensely,' replied the patient.

The doctor lifted the patient's index finger and placed it on his thigh. 'Is it paining here?'

'Ugh ... ugh ... ugh ... Doctor! It is unbearable on the thigh,'
responded the patient.

The doctor then lifted his finger and placed it on his stomach.
'What about here?' he asked.

'Ouu ... ui ... ui ... I cannot tolerate the shooting pain.'

The doctor then made the patient look at his index finger. It had
a wooden splinter stuck on it. The finger itself was the problem,
not the rest of the body. But with his aching finger as the gauge,
the whole body seemed to be hurting.

Similarly, if our mind is preoccupied with the shortcomings
of our family members, the defects of the boss, potholes in
the roads and meanness of relatives, it is highly likely that our
mindset is faulty, due to which the world appears defective to
us.

You may have heard the story of the grumpy old lady who
would always complain to her husband about her neighbours.

'Look, my dear!' she would lament. 'They have the worst
hygiene sense in the world. Their car is so dirty. How come they
never wash it?' Another day she would say, 'Darling, see the
clothes on our neighbours' washing line. They have big blotches
on them. Could they not see the dirt while washing?' Sometimes,
she would complain about the wall, 'Who can be messier than our
neighbours? Even the walls of their home have stains on them.'

One beautiful morning, the old lady awoke and peeped out
of her window. She was astonished to find everything clean. 'My
dear husband, what happened suddenly to them today? Their
walls, clothes and car are all so clean!'

'Nothing has changed in their lifestyle, my dear,' the husband responded. 'Last night, before sleeping, I cleaned our windowpanes.'

As hilarious and absurd as it may seem, it was merely the dirt on her own windowpanes that was making the old lady perceive the outside world as dirty.

In the same manner, if our mind habitually gravitates towards the defects of others and the shortcomings in our surroundings, and if we have made it a lifetime's pursuit of focussing upon negativities, then we ought to stand back and examine ourselves. 'Is there even a remote possibility that the world is not as defective as I thought, and instead, the shortcoming is in me?'

Consider the example of archery. When the archer misses the mark, does he or she say, 'It's the fault of the bullseye; it's in the wrong place? It should have been on the edge of the target; why is it in the centre?' Certainly not! Failure to hit the bullseye is never the target's fault. The archer takes sole responsibility for the poor shot. And admitting his shortcoming is the first step in becoming a proficient archer.

Likewise, when we accept that our undesirable emotions are a weakness, then, and only then, can we think of progressing from that state. We are then transformed from being negative thinkers—who focus on problems—to positive thinkers—who focus on solutions. With that attitude, even if we worry, we worry effectively. We concern ourselves with finding solutions to the problems we face. And it is by focussing on solutions that we bring excellence to our life.

However, to accept our inadequacies is not an easy task. The deceiving mind always provides new arguments for us to believe otherwise. Hence, some people say, 'The environment is not to blame, but I am also not to blame. There is something else that is the cause of the problems. It is the will of God.' Others say, 'The defect is in my destiny.' Yet others claim, 'It is all the fault of time. My time has not yet come; when it does, I will automatically be transformed.' Know that all these justifications are lame excuses.

Let us now address each of the above pretexts and bring out the fallacy in them. Only then can we develop a firm resolve to take the onus for our moods and valiantly strive to improve them.

Is God the Director of Our Actions?

Is God the actual doer of everything? This doubt lingers even in the minds of many Vedic scholars. In the Mahabharat, the evil Duryodhan had stated this logic for his actions:

> *jānāmi dharmaṁ na cha me pravṛittiḥ*
> *jānāmyadharmaṁ na cha me nivṛittiḥ*
> *kenāpi devena hṛidisthitena*
> *yathā niyuktosmi tathā karomi*

'I know what is right and I know what is wrong. But there is some *devata* (celestial god) sitting inside me. As he provokes me, so I behave.'

Many people argue along similar lines. If they make a mistake and you ask them why it happened, they say, 'It must be the will of God.'

56

'What do you mean?'

'I mean it is God who does everything. We are merely puppets in His hands.' They even use quotations from scriptures to validate their argument.

umā dāru joṣhita kī nāīṅ, sabahi nachāvata rāma gosāīṅ
(Ramayan)

'Just as a puppeteer makes wooden dolls dance, the Lord is making us all dance to His tune.' Therefore, according to these people, the Almighty is responsible for our actions. One sentence very commonly uttered by people is: *binā bhagavān kī kṛipā ke ek pattā bhī nahīṅ hilatā.* 'Without the will of God, not even a leaf can move.'

On hearing this, people become reassured, 'This means God is the doer of all our actions, so we need not bother about improving them.' However, this is deleterious thinking. It needs to be diligently weeded out of our mind. Here are some arguments refuting it:

1. If God were the doer of all our deeds, we would never have committed any mistakes. All our actions would have been perfect, since God can never make a blunder. But the fact that we make innumerable mistakes implies that we are doing things of our own free will.

2. If God were the doer, we would not have to bear any karmic reactions for our actions. Why would we suffer for actions that God performed through us? He would either bear the karmic results on His own or forgive Himself. However, there is the Law of Karma which states:

karama pradhāna visva kari rākhā
    jo jasa karai so tasa phalu chākhā   (Ramayan)

'The world is under the wheel of karma. What we do is what we get.' The same law is stated in the Bible as well:

Do not be deceived: God cannot be mocked. A man reaps what he sows.   (Galatians 6:7)

The existence of the Law of Karma implies that we are the doers of our actions.

3. God is impartial towards all souls and perfectly just. If He were the doer of our actions, He would make us all behave equally. Either He would make everyone do good deeds so that they would become saints, or He would make everyone do misdeeds and turn them into demons. However, as we know, there is so much disparity in the world. One person is a saint, like Prahlad, while another is a demon, like Hiranyakashipu. This variety implies that we have the freedom to choose our own thoughts and actions. We alone are responsible for them, not God.

4. If God were the inspirer of our actions, there would be no need for Him to reveal the Vedas or any other scriptures. He would not need to explain the path of perfection to us. He would have simply said: 'O souls, I am the doer of everything. So, you do not need to understand proper and improper action.' Yet, even at the end of the Bhagavad Gita, Lord Krishna underscores the importance of action based on proper knowledge, and states:

iti te jñānam ākhyātaṁ guhyād guhyataraṁ mayā
vimṛiśhyaitad aśheṣheṇa yathechchhasi tathā kuru

(18.63)

'O Arjun, I have given you divine knowledge. Now, contemplate upon it deeply, and then do as you wish.' Similarly, Lord Ram delivered a discourse to the residents of Ayodhya. He said to them:

sunahu karahu jo tuhmahi sohāī (Ramayan)

'Hear Me out and then do as you wish.'

There are some places in the Vedic scriptures where God is called the doer. But their context must be understood very carefully to avoid confusion. The matter will become clear if we can comprehend two terms: *prayojak kartā* and *prayojya kartā*.

- **Prayojak kartā** is the one who bestows the power to perform actions. God is the prayojak kartā, for He provides our senses, mind and intellect with the power for action.
- **Prayojya kartā** is the one who uses the power. The individual soul is the prayojya kartā, for it utilises this power.

For example, the power plant provides electricity to individual homes. How they utilise it is their choice. Similarly, God energises the eyes with the power of vision. After that, what we see is a choice we make. We could either visit a temple and see the divine form of God or we could sit in a movie theatre and watch a movie. In either case, it is our choice and we cannot blame God for it. We cannot say, 'Why does the good Lord always show me movies?' He only bestows on us the power of sight; how we utilise it is left to our discretion.

Having given us the power to work, the second thing that God does is to note the actions we perform and provide us the karmic reactions. The problem arises because when there are negative consequences, we complain, 'Why did the Lord do this to me?'

'God did not do it.'

'Then who did it?'

'God did it, you are right. But He did not do it arbitrarily. He only gave you the results of your actions.'

Compare this with a judge sentencing the accused to prison. The convict may complain that the judge was prejudiced against him. But the judge would respond that he was not the convict's enemy; he was only doing his duty. The evidence of the crime had been established. He only gave the verdict according to the law, to correct the defective behaviour of the criminal and prevent him from repeating such an act in the future.

We must therefore not blame God for our actions. If we made a mistake, we need to take responsibility for it and then improve ourselves to ensure it is not repeated in the future. Yet again, to accept the onus for our inadequacies is not an easy task. People bring another alibi into the picture. They blame destiny for it. We will take that up next.

The Role of Destiny in Our Life

Many people have the staunch belief that their life is governed by destiny. They provide various arguments to support their views.

yaddhātrā nija bhāla paṭṭa likhitaṁ stokaṁ mahaddvādhanaṁ
tatprāpnoti marusthalepi natarāṁ merau tato nādhikam
taddhīro bhava vitta vatsu kṛpaṇāṁ vṛittiṁ vṛithā mā kṛithāḥ
kūpe paśyapayo nidhāvapi ghaṭo ghṛṇāti tulyaṁ jalam

'Whether you immerse a pot in a well or in an ocean, it will get filled with the same volume of water. Similarly, you will only get as much wealth as is written in the pot of your destiny. Living on the golden Sumeru Mountain will not help you get more, and residing in the desert will not make you get less. Thus, putting in any effort is futile.'

Above, I have merely repeated the statement of some fatalists. To think that we are bound by our destiny, which cannot be changed, is the doctrine of fatalism. This is how fatalism is defined:

1. **Doctrine of fate**: The philosophy according to which all events are fated to happen and human beings cannot change their destiny.
2. **Belief in all-powerful fate**: The notion that people cannot influence the future or their own actions.
3. **Feeling of powerlessness against fate**: An attitude of resignation and passivity that results from the belief that people are helpless against Providence.

We will analyse whether the tenets of fatalism are correct or not, but first, let us understand the concept of destiny. The scriptures state:

pūrva janma kṛitaṁ karma taddaivamiti kathyate
(Hitopadeśh)

'The actions we performed in our past lives created our destiny in the present life.' In other words, destiny is not something that came down from the heavens. Nor is it the horoscope read by astrologers. We created our destiny through our actions in past births. This means that in our past lifetimes, we performed actions by exercising our free will.

We shall now use the technique of *Reductio ad absurdum* to disprove fatalism. This is a method where the statement to be invalidated is accepted as the premise. Then it is shown to lead to a logical inconsistency. Let us start with the premise that everything is predestined.

- If we are bound by destiny in this life and cannot perform actions of our own volition, then this rule must have existed in our past lives as well.
- It would mean that even in our previous lives we were bound by destiny, for the rule must be the same for all our lives.
- But, if in each life we were bound by fate, then in which life did we perform independent actions that created the destiny?
- If we never performed actions based on free will in our previous lives, then how was destiny created?

- Again, if we acted by exercising our free will in any past life, then we can do so in our present life as well.

Thus, the premise that everything is predestined leads to a logical absurdity and is negated. The Ramayan states:

daiva daiva ālasī pukārā

'It is lazy people who blame destiny for their substandard achievements.'

It is a fact that there is an element of destiny. But that is a creation of our past karmas. The Vedic scriptures explain three kinds of karmas:

- *Sañchit* karmas
- *Prārabdh* karmas
- *Kriyamāṇ* karmas

Sañchit karmas is the stockpile of our karmas of countless lifetimes. God keeps an account of it. At the time of our birth, when He sends us into the world, He gives us a portion of our sañchit karmas to enjoy and suffer. This is called prārabdh karma. The prārabdh is fixed for the present life. But at every moment, we also have the freedom to act as we choose. These are called kriyamāṇ karma—the actions we perform in the present life of our free will. The prārabdh is predetermined, but kriyamāṇ is not predetermined. It is in our hands and can be changed as we wish.

Compare this to a game of cards. The hand that is dealt to us gets fixed—it cannot be changed. But how we play with the cards is not pre-decided. Good players win even with bad cards, while bad players lose even with good hands.

In the same way, if you were destined to win a jackpot of a million dollars, you would win it. But beyond that, it is your self-effort. On the one hand, if you work hard, you could multiply it into ten million dollars; it would be your *puruṣārth* (self-effort). On the other hand, if you develop wasteful habits, you could squander it away in drinking and gambling. That would not be the fault of your destiny; it would be your imprudence.

The Science of Astrology

In both the Eastern and Western worlds, the science of astrology is extremely popular, for it claims to predict our destiny. Hence, many people approach astrologers to know their future. Predictions according to zodiac signs are popular columns in many magazines as well. But is it authentic, and should we spend time showing our horoscope to astrologers?

The first thing to bear in mind regarding astrology is that the predictions are only partially accurate. In Kaliyug, the present age, there are practically no expert astrologers. With their rudimentary knowledge, they make guesses. A small portion of their predictions turns out right and keeps them in business. I remember a confession about this:

In the 1970s, Khushwant Singh was the editor of Illustrated Weekly, *which was at that time India's number one news magazine. His astrologer, who wrote the zodiac predictions of the week, had left the job. Thence onwards, for the next three years, Khushwant Singh did not hire another astrologer. He would write the predictions himself. Unaware of this, people would often pay compliments about the accuracy of the astrological forecasts in his magazine. Only much later did Khushwant Singh confess that the zodiac predictions used to be concocted by him.*

The second point regarding astrology is that even if the predictions happen to be accurate, they are usually disadvantageous to know. Let us suppose an astrologer informs you that after two years your business will increase manifold. On hearing this, your natural response will be, 'Oh, is that so? Then I do not need to work hard. I am going to succeed in any case.' In other words, when you come to know your future is promising, you will reduce your efforts to achieve success.

Now, consider what will happen if the astrologer tells you, 'Your business will crash after ten years.' On hearing it, you will think, 'Really, my business is going to crash? Oh God, what will I do? What will I do? ...' Whether the business crashes or not, excessive worrying will make your heart crash!

In this way, when a rosy future is predicted, we become lazy, and when the prediction is negative, we become worried. Therefore, there is no advantage in knowing our destiny. Whatever is written in our fate, we will get it by itself. Only the present is in our hands, and we must put in our best efforts—in the here and now. Let us focus on *making* our destiny rather than *knowing* it!

We possess the free will to change our future with our puruṣhārth. The problem with studying astrology is that it makes us fatalistic. We lose focus on our efforts. Hence, Chanakya, the legendary political advisor of the great King Chandragupta Maurya, said:

nirutsāhāddaivaṁ patitaḥ

'If you are lazy in your endeavour, despite the best of destiny, you will fail.'

utsāhavatāṁ śhatravopi vaśhībhavanti

'If you strive earnestly, you can transform even bad destiny into success.'

Therefore, a good policy is to take the predictions of astrologers with a pinch of salt and focus on our efforts. The famous Urdu poet, Allama Muhammad Iqbal, put it very aptly:

khudī ko karbuland itanā ki har takadīr se pahale
khudā khud bande se pūchhe batā terī razā kyā hai

'Make your exertions so strong, that before giving you the results of your fate, God Himself asks, "What do you want?"'

The Time to Act Is Now!

If destiny is also not to blame, then what is? Time! Many believe time is all-powerful. They are of the view that the passage of time will bring us to perfection automatically, hence we can simply relax and wait for that time to come. They say:

puruṣha balī nahīṅ hota hai, samaya hota balavān
bhilaiṅ lūṭīṅ gopikā, soi arjun soi bān

'Humans are not powerful; time is omnipotent. Look at Arjun. He had the same weapons with which he fought the Mahabharat, and yet, when the time came, ordinary tribal thieves stole the gopis from his custody.'

Is this understanding correct? Will the time come when we will improve our thinking? Wrong again! The time will not come when our mind and thoughts will automatically become pure; rather, time is passing by. No moment that goes by will ever return. Before we know it, the time we have to live on this planet will have slipped through our fingers like grains of sand. We must fully utilise the moments at our disposal by exerting our every sinew. Thus, the scriptures state:

ālasyaṁ hi manuṣhyāṇāṁ śharīrastho mahān ripuḥ

'The biggest affliction in the human body is the disease of laziness.' We shroud it in various robes.

- There is a breed of people who say, 'I am getting ready.' A year later, you ask them, and they are still getting ready. They do not realise it, but they are suffering from a disease called 'procrastination'.

- There are those who say they will do it one of these days. You can be sure they will do it none of these days.

- Another type waits for all the traffic lights to turn green before they start from home. They suffer from the disease of 'excusitis'.

- And yet another group, on being urged to take action, pronounces, 'I am analysing.' The problem is that six months later, they are still analysing. They are afflicted by the phenomenon of 'paralysis by analysis'.

The secret of success lies in rejecting all such unproductive thoughts and using the present moment to the best of our ability. That is the way to build a successful future.

The Transformational Power of Puruṣhārth

Puruṣhārth is the self-effort we put in the present, utilising the free will that God has bestowed upon us. Let us imbibe the spirit of puruṣhārth from Mahakavi Kalidas, one of the greatest poets in the history of Sanskrit literature:

In his childhood, Kalidas was no prodigy. In fact, he was quite the reverse. A famous story describes that once he was cutting the very branch that he was sitting upon! He did not realise that he would fall. In that position, he was spotted by some pandits of that kingdom.

The pandits had a score to settle with a princess. She was extremely beautiful and had put forth a condition for marriage—she would only marry the scholar who could defeat her in śhāstrārth (scriptural debate). Many scholars had been enticed by her beauty and had engaged in discussion with her, but she had defeated all of them. This made them sore, and they connived to teach her a lesson by getting her married to the biggest dunce.

That was the time they spotted Kalidas. They asked him to climb down the tree. They told him, 'We will solve your problem of poverty forever if you do as we say.' With his consent, they dressed him up, tied an ornamental turban around his head and took him to the palace.

'O Princess, we have in our presence a great scholar from Kashi. He wishes to engage in debate with you but is presently observing the vow of silence. Thus, he will only debate with gestures.' The princess audaciously agreed.

The two of them sat facing each other. The princess raised her right hand, lifting one finger. Kalidas was already feeling threatened in the ominous environment. Seeing her raised finger, he concluded that she was implying, 'I will poke one of your eyes.' In response, he raised two fingers, indicating, 'I will poke both your eyes.'

The scholars asked the princess, 'What was your question?'

She said, 'I asked whether the Supreme Divine Entity is one or many.'

The pandits replied, 'The great scholar raised two fingers to indicate that the Supreme is both formless and with form, hence, He is two.'

Next, the princess raised her five fingers. Kalidas thought she was threatening to slap him. In return, he raised his fist, expressing, 'I will punch you.'

The pandits again asked, 'O Princess, what was your question?'

She said, 'I asked that the five senses are troubling the soul; what is the solution?'

The pandits responded, 'The great scholar responded by lifting his fist. He was indicating that the mind must be used to rein in the tumultuous senses.'

In this way, the debate proceeded. Helped by his silence, the pandits made Kalidas win. Since the princess had given her word, she married him.

One day, after the wedding, both husband and wife were sitting on the patio of their palace, when a camel (uṣṭra) went by. Seeing it, Kalidas exclaimed, 'Utra ... utra ... utra ...,' unable to say the proper Sanskrit word.

The princess was shocked and looked at him in dismay. 'He seems to be illiterate. The pandits have deceived me.' She was so upset that she pushed Kalidas down the flight of stairs. He fell cartwheeling down and hit the ground with a thud.

There was a temple of Mother Kali nearby. He offered his prayers there and resolved, 'If vidyā (learning) is so important to the princess, then a scholar is what I will become.' He arose and went to Kashi, the city of scholars, where he acquired immense knowledge.

Many years later, he returned, an erudite scholar. He knocked on his wife's door and said authoritatively: kapāṭaṁ dwāram dehi. *'My dear wife, please open the door.'*

His wife heard him; she was impressed by the command in his voice and the confidence in his words. She responded: asti kaśhchit vāgviśheṣhaḥ. *'It seems you have become a master of speech and expression.'*

The great Kalidas used the three words his wife uttered at that historic moment of reunion to start three of his *mahākāvyas* (great works of poetry) that reign supreme in Sanskrit literature even today.

- With *asti-uttarasyāṁ diśi,* he began his epic *Kumāra-sambhavam.*
- With *kaścit kāntā,* he started his magnum opus poem, *Meghdūta.*
- His epic, *Raghuvaṁśa,* begins with *vāgarthhāviva.*

This is the power of self-effort. It transformed a dunce into a 'mahakavi', a great poet. If Kalidas had blamed destiny, the will of God, or the passage of time for his previous lack of education, he would never have put in the intense exertion that changed his life. But Kalidas did not fall victim to the blame game. He realised that his present condition was a consequence of past actions. If he continued to perform the same actions, his future would remain the same. Since he wished his life to be different, he grabbed the present moment and worked hard to make the change.

Likewise, we must not fall victim to the temptation of playing the blame game. We must not hold destiny, God or time responsible for our actions. We must also refrain from being obsessed with problems, and instead, apply ourselves to finding the appropriate solutions.

Thus, taking responsibility for our situation in life is the second mindset for success, happiness and fulfilment. With it, we begin to put in the effort required for improving ourselves. How can we energize the effort for self-enhancement?

This brings us to the third mindset, which is 'inspiration'. It is the fuel that provides fervour to our aspirations, enthusiasm for our actions and energy to our life. In the next chapter, we will discuss this vital ingredient that will help us in enriching our personality.

CHAPTER 3

THE MINDSET OF INSPIRATION

In the previous chapter, we discussed the mindset of responsibility. When we are equipped with it, we make no excuses for our inadequacies. Instead, we accept our shortcomings and focus on solutions to help us progress. Now, improvement requires enthusiastic effort and vigorous action. This brings us to the third mindset for success, which is the mindset of inspiration.

Inspiration connects us with an inexhaustible resource of energy within ourselves. It is the fuel that powers our efforts and lifts us up the mountain of material and spiritual success. It adds intensity to our thoughts and quality to our efforts. When we do not feel inspired even a noble activity seems boring and tedious. But when inspired, we complete even a routine activity with devotion and dedication. Veritably, a moment of inspired living is worth a lifetime spent in insipidity. Hence, the saying: 'Life is not measured by the number of breaths we take, but by the moments that take our breath away.'

From inspiration springs 'motivation', which literally means 'motive for action'. It is the passion we bring to our work, life, attitude and effort for self-improvement. It immediately makes us stand out in the crowd.

Consider the case of Utsav, a teenager. His summer vacation had started, and he thought of getting a job during the break. Going through the advertisements, he saw one from the biggest mall in the neighbourhood. He submitted his neatly typed job application. Soon he was delighted to receive an invitation for the job interview at 9 a.m. the following Monday.

On Monday, filled with enthusiasm, Utsav reached the mall office at 8.30 a.m., only to discover that twenty job aspirants were already waiting ahead of him. He was the twenty-first in line. This was very discouraging. What chance did he stand? The manager would probably be exhausted and may have already selected someone by the time his turn came. However, Utsav was an inspired youngster, with an unflagging spirit. He scribbled a note and put it before the clerk in the waiting room. 'Madam,' he said, 'Can you please hand this to the manager? It is an urgent matter.'

The lady clerk snubbed him, 'Sonny, wait in the line. Your turn to meet the boss will come, and then you can hand it to him.'

'Madam,' Utsav urged, 'This is very important. It needs to be handed to him now.'

The old lady was experienced, and something in Utsav's voice convinced her. She took his note and handed it to the manager. He had written, 'Sir, I am the twenty-first applicant in line. Decide nothing until you see me.' Utsav's enthusiasm was insuppressible.

The manager did not fail to realise that Utsav had a vital ingredient for success at work. His enthusiasm made him stand out in the group and bag the job.

For the Inspired, No Problem Is Too Big

No endeavour is free from difficulties, and the higher the goal, the bigger the obstacles on the way. What makes some continue optimistically while others lose heart? Inspiration is, again, the propellant that keeps us going in the face of our biggest challenges in life. H.W. Arnold put it very well:

> The worst bankrupt in the world is the man who has lost his enthusiasm. Let a man lose everything else in the world but enthusiasm and he will come through again to success.

If one does not possess the zeal for progress, then even a small problem will appear like a mountain. And if one is sincerely inspired to reach the goal, then even the toughest challenge will seem puny. This was amply illustrated in the life of Soichiro Honda, founder of the Honda automotive empire.

Soichiro Honda was not born with the proverbial golden spoon in his mouth. Rather, he had very humble beginnings. His father was a blacksmith and ran a small bicycle repair shop. Young Soichiro would sometimes help his father at the shop. As his love for automobiles grew, the fifteen-year-old Soichiro dropped out of school and took up a job at a renowned auto repair garage in Tokyo. He worked there relentlessly for six years as an apprentice, improving his knowledge and skills. Then, he returned home and started his own auto repair business, which picked up within no time. However, his thirst for innovation was not quenched. He created a new design for piston rings and presented it to Toyota Corporation. His design was rejected, as only three out of fifty rings could pass the quality test, but that did not stop him. He started researching, visiting several manufacturers and even joined an engineering institute. This made him the butt of ridicule amongst his friends. 'You were dreaming of selling piston rings to Toyota Corporation?' they jeered at him.

However, the fountain source of inspiration within Honda was so irrepressible that he refused to get discouraged. With the newly acquired knowledge, he went back to the drawing board to work on his design. After a few attempts, his design was selected. Toyota Corporation placed a large order for piston rings and extended him the capital for constructing his factory. Along with a few friends, he set up his manufacturing units. His company was a grand success and employed about two thousand people during its peak.

In the meantime, the bombing of Pearl Harbor happened, and as a result, Japan and the US were at war. Honda's factory was flattened during a bombing. All cement supply was now diverted to Japan's war effort and there was none left for reconstructing the plant.

The factory had been bombed, but not Mr Honda's enthusiasm. He created a new method for manufacturing cement and reconstructed the factory a second time, using the gasoline containers that the US planes had dropped during their bombing sorties. Unfortunately, soon after the factory was ready, it got levelled again by a high-intensity earthquake in Japan. This threw Honda totally out of business.

Later that year, the war ended with Japan's defeat. Fuel was now in short supply all over Japan. People did not have fuel to drive their cars, and so the sale of Toyota cars had fallen to zero. Poor Mr Honda did not even have fuel for his car. As a diversion, he fitted a motor to his bicycle and created the first motorcycle. It caught the fancy of his neighbours and they asked him to fit motors to their cycles as well. After he had made a few dozen motorcycles, he thought it was a marketable idea.

Note his enthusiasm! He obtained a list of eight thousand bicycle dealers in Japan. He handwrote a business proposal to five thousand of them. Eighteen hundred responded and extended the capital for the startup. He set up a plant and produced the first factory-made motorcycle. It was poorly received, for it was too big. Still, Honda did not give up. He created a smaller version, and it was an immediate success. After that, Soichiro Honda never looked back. The Honda empire became global and, within his lifetime itself, employed one hundred thousand people worldwide. It has grown even further since then.

The key to Honda's success was the mindset of enthusiasm. This is the attitude that helps one cut through difficulties as a knife cuts through butter. If people lose everything in life but their inspiration, they can gain it all back again. But if inspiration is lost, everything will be lost. It is thus the elixir that keeps one strong even in difficult times.

The journey of spiritual elevation is an equally arduous one. We will have to face colossal difficulties and scale immense heights. Through it all, inspiration is the insurance policy that will ensure we do not give up. Maharshi Patanjali, one of the greatest sages of Vedic philosophy, stated:

tīvra saṁvegānāmāsannaḥ   (*Patañjali Yog Darśhan* 1.21)

'Endeavour for spiritual elevation with great energy.' In the Bible, Jesus gave his followers the same advice:

So, because you are lukewarm—neither hot nor cold—I am about to spit you out of my mouth.   (Revelations 3.16)

We have seen the importance of motivation in success in both material and spiritual realms of activity. Let us now understand the science of motivation.

Is Inspiration a Gift That Some Are Born With?

How can we enthuse ourselves and access that immense powerhouse within us? Are some persons born with an inspired mindset or can it be developed? The following story will answer this question:

A factory worker used to walk to work every day. His plant was an hour away from his home. He worked the evening shift that was from 4 p.m. to 12 midnight. After the shift, he would walk back and reach home by 1 a.m.

The path between the factory and his home went around a large cemetery. In order to find a shorter route, one night he ventured into the graveyard. The shortcut saved him twenty minutes, and nothing untoward happened; there were no scary sightings of ghosts and spirits. So, he decided that the shortcut was an attractive option. Subsequently, he began walking through the graveyard every night.

One day, a new grave had been dug in the middle of the path. It was a dark moonless night. As he was walking through the graveyard, unaware, he fell headlong into the pit. Sitting in it, he realised he had fallen into a freshly dug grave. He tried hoisting himself out. However, its walls were a full eight feet high, and he could not lift himself out. He resigned to the idea of spending the night there, waiting for some passerby to discover him the next morning.

It so happened that he was not the only tresspasser in the graveyard that night. Twenty minutes went by and a drunkard came along the same path. He was too inebriated to see the newly dug grave and fell headlong into it. Stunned, he realised that he was lying in a grave in the dead of the night, and it scared him. What if there were ghosts and spirits around? He desperately tried to scramble out of the grave but without success.

Sitting in the other end of the grave, the factory worker had seen the drunkard fall in and was observing his vain efforts to climb out. To offer a word of sympathetic advice, he approached the drunkard from behind, and put his hand on his back. 'It is no use, my friend; you cannot get out of here ...'

This was the scariest moment in the drunkard's life. Here he was trying to climb out of the grave, and an unknown creature behind him was telling him that he could not get out. He realised that he was in deep trouble, with no help or support. He suddenly found the motivation to put in superhuman effort and yanked himself out. Before the person behind could complete his sentence, he was out of the grave.

The story illustrates how motivation changes with situations. Factory managers grumble that their workers are not enthused but look at the same workers when they get out of the factory on a Friday evening. There is a spring in their step and a song on their lips. It shows that they do possess enthusiasm, though it is not for work. Often parents complain that their children are not motivated, but is that also true when they pack their stuff for a weekend trip? They do possess motivation, just that it is not for studies.

Thus, we too, and others we interact with, can be inspired if we know the secret.

A devotee once approached me with a problem. He said, 'Swami-ji, I am getting frustrated because of a human relations problem in business. My subordinate's performance is substandard, and it is impacting our company. I have often threatened to fire him, but he makes an emotional appeal about how his old parents are dependent upon him, and he will have no means of supporting them if he loses the job. I am in a dilemma. What should I do?'

I said, 'Instead of firing him out, try firing him up. Fill him with enthusiasm for the work.' I taught him a few points by which he would be able to inspire his subordinate. A month later, the devotee came back to me and said, 'Swami-ji, you were right! He has changed so much. The level at which he is performing, he is a role model for the team. I would not lose him for anything.'

Let us now see how we can ignite such immense motivation in others and ourselves.

What Are the Factors That Demotivate Us?

Organisational psychologists have studied the reasons that negatively impact people's enthusiasm for work in corporations. The main factors they come up with are:

- Seeing a non-performer rewarded
- Failure or fear of failure
- Negative criticism
- Lack of direction
- Responsibility without authority
- Poor quality standards
- Lack of measurable objectives
- Lack of priorities
- Unfair treatment
- Frequent change of instructions
- Public humiliation

The above list makes sense. Experience tells us that these factors do impact people negatively. For that reason, they must be carefully avoided in personnel management.

Nevertheless, the science of motivation is not so simple. These very factors, which are demotivating for some, can be catalysts for motivation in others. This is why you also hear people making statements like:

- 'My colleague was unfairly promoted over me. I will now work twice as hard to show them that he is no better than me.'
- 'She criticised my performance. Now I will succeed so tremendously that she will have to eat her words.'

- 'My worth is not being recognised by my organisation. I will toil so hard that I will show them what I am made of.'
- 'I was publicly humiliated. I will transform my life and prove myself to those who laughed at me today.'

The same situations that prove uninspiring for some are inspiring for others. Is the science of motivation very ambiguous? We need to probe this further.

Research done on two brothers led to similarly perplexing findings:

Two brothers were living in Toronto, Canada. The elder brother's life was in shambles. He was a drug addict; he would drink enough to be able to float a ship; he was a wife beater; he could never stick to any job he got; he had even spent time in prison for attacking his boss.

On the other hand, his younger brother seemed to have a perfect life. He had good health, well-behaved children, a well-paying job, satisfied bosses and helpful neighbours.

Social scientists were curious to know how two brothers, growing up in the same environment, were so different in their ways. They asked the elder one why he seemed to have failed in life.

'What else could I do?' the elder brother responded. 'My father was a drunkard and died of cirrhosis of the liver at the age of thirty-eight. While growing up, I saw him getting drunk every day, creating a ruckus and beating the family members. Having been raised in such a miserable family environment, it was natural that I also followed suit.'

The social scientists commiserated. 'He is right. It is the fault of his upbringing.' They then asked his younger brother how his life was such a success.

'How could I ever become a drunkard?' the younger brother retorted. 'While growing up, I saw my father getting drunk every day. He ruined his health, lost his job and destroyed the peace at home. Seeing the mistakes he made, there was no way I could repeat them in my life.'

The social scientists again commiserated. 'He is right. He learnt the lessons by observing the mistakes made by his father.'

The two brothers had grown up in the same family and had been exposed to exactly the same situations. Yet, the elder brother was demotivated by them, while the younger brother was highly inspired to lead a better life.

What, then, is the secret of motivation? If you Google this question, you will only come up with shallow behavioural tips—dos and don'ts. These are all helpful but very superficial. Unfortunately, it seems that this vitally important science of motivation is quite a mystery the world over. Let us now unravel it step by step. Make sure you follow the logic all the way through.

Internal vs External Motivation

People get inspired in contrasting ways. For some, the external reward is the fuel that enthuses them. For example, if their boss praises them, they become motivated; if their efforts are visible to society, they feel inspired. Thus, their impetus for motivation is external. The problem with such a mindset is that, if tomorrow their boss criticises them, they will become discouraged. If their achievements are not highlighted in society, they will be dispirited.

In other words, external rewards hold the key to their enthusiasm. For them to become immensely motivated, something needs to happen on the outside. However, the downside here is that the same key can also be used in the reverse direction, to switch off their passion.

In contrast there are the internally motivated people. They create inspiring thoughts, values, beliefs and goals within themselves. Whether the external circumstances are favourable or unfavourable is immaterial to them. They possess the ability to tap into an inner source of passion that propels them to excellence, achievement and success.

Such internally motivated people are insulated from fluctuating external conditions. Adverse circumstances and negative people do not dishearten them. Hence, always brimming with enthusiasm, they easily surf over the turbulent waves of the ocean of life.

To elaborate on this point, I would like to share a personal lesson in inner motivation that was taught to me by my spiritual master.

Under Jagadguru Shree Kripalu-ji Maharaj's tutelage, I began studying the Vedic scriptures. He wanted me to spread this knowledge for the well-being of others in the future.

As a service to him, I dived deep into the study of the ancient books of wisdom, like the Upanishads and Puranas. Since I did not have experience in oratory, I thought it would be advantageous to practise public speaking as well. The only hitch was that there was no public in the ashram (monastery). So, I would practise lecturing to the wall. But nothing can be more uninspiring than staring into a stark wall and sharing the subtle nuances of Vedic philosophy with it.

I went up to my guru and requested, 'Maharaj-ji, can you please depute a resident of the ashram to sit and listen to me speak for one-and-a-half hours every day?' That was an unreasonable request because the handful of ashram locals who lived there were all busy with their respective duties.

However, Maharaj-ji utilised that opportunity to teach me an invaluable lesson. He said, 'My child, lack of inspiration or carelessness does not come from the outside. It originates from within and can be eradicated from within as well.'

Maharaj-ji then went on to teach me a mantra from the Vedas:

sa yathā kāmo bhavati tat kratur bhavati
yat kratur bhavati tat karma kurute
yat karma kurute tad abhiniṣ padyate

The mantra states that if you create an intense desire within yourself, you will make a firm resolve. Then you will put in immense effort and achieve stellar progress. But if your desire is mild, then the resolve will be feeble. And if the resolve is weak, then your effort will be marginal and your progress poor.

Maharaj-ji instructed me to remember the above formula for life. I then understood that the carelessness I was experiencing was coming from within, and it was in my capacity to eliminate it. As a result, with a firm resolve, I applied myself to my work and was able to deliver a supercharged lecture to a blank wall. After that, I found I could do the same to the cornfields around the ashram, the trees, sheep, cows, an irrigation canal and anything under the sun. I seemed to have unplugged an inestimable supply of inner inspiration. For the entire year that I lived in the ashram while reading the scriptures, I gave lectures every day to a non-existing audience with unbounded enthusiasm.

Thus, we see how internal motivation is more reliable than external motivation. It is independent of the environment and always at our beck and call. If we can access it, we will discover an inexhaustible powerhouse of energy within ourselves.

What, then, is the way to motivate ourselves internally?

The Key to Internal Motivation

We become motivated to strive for our goals when we have compelling reasons: 'Why do I need to do this?', 'What will I gain from this activity?' or 'What will I lose if I do not accomplish the goal?' This is true for all goals, whether related to work, diet, self-improvement or the like. Here is an anecdote illustrating the above principle:

A salesman from Delhi reached Shimla to sell his wares. He spent the night in a wayside inn. Next morning, he discovered there had been heavy snowfall throughout the night and the road was white with it.

The salesman asked the innkeeper, 'Do you think I will be able to go out and sell my goods in these conditions?'

The innkeeper replied, 'Sir, that depends on whether you work on commission or salary.'

This is indeed a true analysis of the situation. A salesperson working on a salary will find very little motivation to brave the snow to reach prospective customers. But one working on commission will get paid for every item sold, and thus will have ample reason to remain motivated even in inclement weather. Here is a second story highlighting the same principle:

A king in medieval Europe was shocked to discover the infidelity of his queen. She was having an affair with a menial palace servant. The king decided to handle the matter tactfully. Rather than punishing the queen, he decided to redeem his honour from the servant.

The servant was brought to the king's court and his deed was exposed. The king then delivered his judgement. 'I have decided to give you one chance to save your life. You and I will engage in a duel. If you defeat me, you will be condoned. Else, you will die by the edge of my sword.' The king thought that the servant had no training in arms. Hence, defeating him would be child's play.

Both donned their armours and lifted their swords and shields. The duel began. Much to the king's chagrin, the servant was no pushover. His mental focus was razor-sharp. He was anticipating the king's moves and parrying them easily. His nimbleness on the feet was so remarkable that it took the king by surprise. Even the power in his blows was unsettling.

Slowly but surely, the king was getting overpowered. Fifteen minutes through the duel, he realised that he would lose. He used his authority to end the fight. 'Stop!' he said. 'I forgive you. You can leave my palace. But do not let me see you in my kingdom again.'

Later, the king asked his commander-in-chief, 'How in the world did the servant put up such a show? I had thought this would be a cakewalk.'

'I doubted it from the beginning, Your Highness,' said the commander-in-chief. 'For you, it was a mere sport. You did not have the motivation to perform. But for the servant, it was a matter of life and death. He had a strong reason to put in his best as he was fighting for dear life. So, I had expected that it would not be easy for you.'

The story offers us an insight into the secret of motivation. The servant had a strong reason to want to win. It was a matter of survival, and he could not afford to lose. The king, on the other hand, had practically no motivation to put in his best effort. For him, it was a mere sport.

The way, then, to get internally motivated is to have a strong 'why' for doing something. If you wish to be inspired to follow a healthy diet, then become convinced about its benefits. And also become fully convinced about the harm by not adhering to it. The strong 'why' will generate the inner push to help you follow the strict diet regimen.

Similarly, to become inspired for a rigorous exercise schedule, find a strong motive for it. Write down the various benefits that you will accrue from regular exercise. Additionally, write down the different ways you could suffer if you do not exercise. If you have a strong enough reason, you will become enthusiastic about it.

It now seems that we have unravelled the secret of inspiration. Do you know what it is? We become motivated to perform an action when we are convinced with solid 'whys' and 'wherefores' of the benefits of it.

And yet, we find that this understanding is still incomplete. A strong answer to 'why' is also not enough. Very often, we know why a diet is necessary, we know what the benefits of regular exercise are, and yet we do not adhere to it. Despite knowing the facts, we still succumb to laziness or go on an eating binge.

Doesn't this happen all the time? There is a vast chasm between what we know and what we do. Thus, even a strong reason is not sufficient for one to act. Why? Obviously, there must be something more to the puzzle of motivation.

Activating the Proper Knowledge in the Intellect

Let us understand how the human intellect works. It is like a vessel that contains various kinds of information on any subject. All that we hear, all that we read and all that we observe gets filled in it. Thus, the intellect contains several pieces of knowledge on any topic. Whichever piece we pick up, that segment of knowledge gets activated.

For example, we may know the benefits of meditation, and yet do not feel enthusiastic about practising it, because the knowledge is dormant. Now, if we bring that knowledge to conscious awareness, it turns on the switch for the fountain source of inspiration. Understand this through a powerful example that I love to share:

The parents of a ten-year-old girl called Lalita were anxious because she did not apply herself to her studies. They asked her the reason for it. Lalita responded by saying that her mind was unable to focus on studies—it kept wandering in all directions. Both, she and her parents, were worried about the problem.

However, when the same Lalita sat for her exams, she brought her mind under control. She focussed on answering the question paper for three hours without getting distracted by anything. When the time was up, the examiner had to snatch the answer sheet away from her.

How did she garner such concentration, when throughout the year she was complaining about the mind being unable to focus on the lessons? This was because her intellect was deeply conscious of the importance of those three hours. She was totally aware that carelessness would result in the loss of an entire year. This forced her mind to apply itself intensely.

If that level of concentration had been maintained all the year round, the girl would probably have turned out to be a national merit scholar. However, through the year, her intellect chose to harbour other ideas, like, 'Studies are not important. They are vital according to my parents, but they do not know anything. They do not understand that playing with my friends is far more critical to me.'

When the decision of the intellect was otherwise, there was no scope for the mind to remain focussed. Even if it did focus for a few moments, the intellect would jerk it away, 'There is no happiness here. Think of your friends; that is where true bliss lies.'

The example above illustrates the extent to which the intellect can direct the mind. The Bhagavad Gita repeatedly refers to this as *Buddhi Yog* (yoga of the intellect). Lord Krishna states:

buddhi-yogam upāśhritya mach-chittaḥ satataṁ bhava

(18.57)

'Taking shelter of the yoga of the intellect, keep your consciousness always absorbed in Me.'

The same principle applies when we wish to find the inspiration to resist temptations. For example, we may wish to reduce the intake of white sugar but find that we lack the self-control. Thus, when the tongue tugs for gratification, we fail to abstain from sweet dishes like gulab jamun and rasgullas.

The way to increase our self-control is to become convinced that white sugar is like poison, and then keep that knowledge in our conscious awareness. We will then discover the inspiration to resist sweet dishes when they are placed before us.

The conclusion is that to become inspired, we must do two things: 1) convince our intellect about the importance of something, and 2) keep the knowledge active by revising and revisiting it repeatedly (*chintan*).

How to Inspire Ourselves on the Spiritual Path

People often express their lack of motivation as a problem to me. They say, 'Swami-ji, nowadays I do not feel enthused about doing my bhakti sadhana (devotional practice). What is the solution for overcoming carelessness?'

Such laziness can be eliminated easily. First, let us understand the cause for the waxing and waning of enthusiasm in devotion. The reason is that the material mind is under the three guṇas (modes of material nature). Hence, the mind is sometimes sāttvic (in the mode of goodness), sometimes rājasic (in the mode of passion) and sometimes tāmasic (in the mode of ignorance).

When the mind is sāttvic, we think, 'I am so blessed to have the human form, and I must make the most of this golden opportunity. Let me apply myself to discipline, sadhana and devotion.'

However, after a while, the mind becomes rājasic. Then we feel, 'I must practise sadhana, but what is the hurry? Let me do it some other time.' Thus, carelessness sets in.

And a little while later, we find ourselves in the tāmasic environment of materialistic friends, TV and movies. Then we think, 'Others are enjoying worldly delights. What is the need for me to deny myself these pleasures? I can practise devotion later in my old age, not now.'

If you experience similar fluctuations in sentiments, do know that this is only natural. Everyone has varying levels of devotional feelings through the day, and from day to day. But that does not mean we are obliged to remain at a lower level of enthusiasm. Rather, we must use our intellect to eliminate the lethargy of the mind, and this is not a long process. **We can shift our mind from being insipid to fervent in just a moment.**

All we need to do is bring proper knowledge to the intellect, and then push the mind to create matching sentiments.

As an example, think of the importance of the human form that we possess. There are 8.4 million species of life in existence. Our soul is transmigrating from lifetime to lifetime through different kinds of bodies.

kabahuṅka kari karunā nara dehī
deta īsha binu hetu sanehī   (Ramayan)

'Very rarely, out of His causeless mercy, the Lord bestows upon the soul the human birth.' It means, in this life we have received a rare blessing that comes once in many births.

Recognise the speciality of what we have received. All creatures are programmed by their genetic structure. When winter comes, birds in the north will only fly south. There is nothing that can make them fly east or west or north. Why? Because they have been programmed by their genes. But we humans have the freedom to choose whether to go north, south, east or west. God has given us the dignity of choice.

Further, we possess the special faculty of knowledge. This enables the power of *vivek* (discerning intellect) that animals do not possess. While humans can be on a quest for knowledge of the Absolute Truth, animals cannot even ponder over the purpose of life.

Humans possess one faculty that even celestial gods do not have. This is the ability for doing puruṣhārth or fruit-bearing karmas (discussed in the previous chapter). We can build upon our karmic account and create our destiny, while celestial beings only reap the rewards of their past karmas. Hence, amongst the 8.4 million species of life, the opportunity to realise God is available exclusively to humans.

However, we should not assume that this body will be reserved for us in the next life as well. The next birth will be determined by our karmas and level of consciousness in this life. Thus, the Vedas state:

iha chedavedīdatha satyamasti
na chedihāvedīnmahatī vinaśhṭhiḥ   (*Kenopaniṣhad* 2.5)

'The human birth is a rare opportunity. If you do not utilise it to achieve your goal, you will suffer great ruin.' Again, they state:

iha chedaśhakad boddhuṁ prākśharīrasya visrasaḥ
tataḥ sargeṣhu lokeṣhu śharīratvāya kalpate
(*Kaṭhopaniṣhad* 2.3.4)

'If you do not strive for God-realisation in this life, you will be stuck in the cycle of life and death for many births.' The Shreemad Bhagavatam states:

nāyaṁ deho deha-bhājāṁ nriloke
kaṣhṭān kāmān arhate viḍ-bhujāṁ ye
tapo divyaṁ putrakā yena sattvaṁ
śhuddhyed yasmād brahma-saukhyaṁ tvanantam
(5.5.1)

'In the human form, one should not undertake great hardships to enjoy sensual pleasures, which are available even to creatures that eat excreta (hogs). Instead, one should practise austerities to purify one's heart, and enjoy the unlimited divine bliss of God.'

The Golden Chance Is Passing Away

Though the human form is a wonderful opportunity the soul has received in this life, we must realise it will not always remain. It will be snatched away in the form of death. Hence, it is temporary. Every single moment of human life is precious and should be put to good use. Chanakya said:

sā hānistanmahachchhidraṁ sa mohaḥ sa vibhramaḥ
yanmuhūrtaṁ kṣhaṇaṁ vāpi vāsudevaṁ na chintayet

'The biggest loss, a colossal misfortune, the darkest illusion and the grossest ignorance is that moment in life which is not used wisely in loving remembrance of Lord Krishna.'

If we can remain aware of the golden chance we have, and how it is slipping away from our hands, we will naturally become inspired to put in our best at every moment in life. This same technique was also used by King Janak, who had elevated himself to the highest spiritual level.

Once upon a time, in the kingdom of Raja Janak, two pandits began discussing the glories of their king. 'Our noble king is famous the world over by the title of "Videha", or the one who is beyond the body,' said the first pandit.

The second pandit responded, 'We are extremely fortunate to be ruled by such a wise and spiritually elevated king.'

'However, I wonder how he manages to remain Videha amid such opulence,' said the first pandit. 'After all, he has a large family and immense luxury at his disposal.'

'Let us go and ask him the secret of his spiritual prowess,' said the second pandit.

The two pandits went to the royal palace and got the audience of the king. 'Your Majesty, we are priests who live in your capital city of Janakpur. We are curious to know how you have become famous as "Videha", though you live amidst such opulence. Can you please share your secret with us?'

King Janak responded as if a snake had bitten him. 'You have the bravado to interrogate your king like this? I order both of you to be hanged at the gallows for this crime. Your punishment will be executed tomorrow. Nevertheless, tonight, my servants will take good care of you. So enjoy yourselves for a short while.'

The two pandits were taken away by the servants. They were bathed with warm water and massaged with scented oil. Clothed in royal attire, they were offered a sumptuous feast. Finally, they were given a luxurious double bed for the night. But sleep was a far cry for them as they lay thinking of their impending death.

The next morning, they were brought to King Janak's court. In a booming voice, the king addressed them, 'I have decided to give you both a chance to save your lives. You will be handed a pot brimming with oil. You will have to carry it around the main marketplace of my capital, Janakpur. If you can make the entire journey without allowing a drop to fall, I will pardon you.'

Both the pandits were taken to the market and handed the vessels plush with oil. Taking each step as softly as possible, with *the utmost focus of their mind and complete absorption of their intellect, they began circumambulating the busy marketplace of Janakpur. Fortunately, both the pandits succeeded in bringing the pots back to the starting point without spilling a drop of oil.*

The guards grabbed them by their arms and propelled them to King Janak. This time, however, the king was smiling. 'You are pardoned,' he said to them. 'But tell me something. Last night, you lived amid such luxury. Did your minds get drawn by temptations and indulge in the pleasures that were available all around you?'

'How could the mind get tempted, Your Majesty?' said the pandits. 'The thought that we would meet our death in the morning was always looming before us.'

'Okay, never mind,' replied the king. 'Today, you walked around the main market of Janakpur. There were many allurements offering a variety of pleasures. Did you get enticed by them?'

'O King, how could we? Our entire focus was on the pot. We had to ensure that not even a drop spilt from it, or it would be the end of us.'

'That is the answer to your question,' King Janak responded. 'You had asked me how I can be Videha while living amidst royal luxuries. The answer is that I always keep my death before me. I remember that life is short, and the golden chance that the human form has created for the soul is transient. That is why I always remain focussed on using every moment judiciously. And my mind does not get enticed by the sensual, materialistic pleasures that surround me.'

Like King Janak, we too can always remain inspired. When we ponder over the value of human life and its transient nature, we will naturally be motivated to do our best. Hence, Jagadguru Kripalu-ji Maharaj stated:

are mana avasara bītyo jāta   (Prem Ras Madira)

'O my dear mind! The golden opportunity you have received is slipping out of your hands. Make the most of it while it lasts.' The poet-saint, Narayan, said:

do bātan ko bhūl mat, jo chāhasi kalyāṇ
nārāyaṇ ika maut ko, dūje śhrī bhagavān

The verse implies that if you wish to make your life a success, then do not forget two things. What should we not forget, God? No, first of all, do not forget your death. And next, remember God. Or else you will keep deferring what needs to be done.

Postponement is the disease that fritters away all our blessings. We get to know from the saints and scriptures what we should do for our welfare. We resolve to do these things as well. But then, we make excuses: 'I will do it later', 'When the time comes, I will do it', 'When I grow old, I will definitely do sadhana', etc. In this way, we make pretexts, and despite all the graces upon us, we do not advance.

Now we must firmly acknowledge and accept that God's abundant grace is already upon us. What is missing is our own grace, i.e. we need to use the grace that has been bestowed upon us. And this requires us to make the most of every moment that we have. Hence, Narad Muni, the celestial sage, stated:

kṣhaṇārdhamapi vyarthaṁ na neyaṁ

(*Nārad Bhakti Darśhan* Sūtra 77)

'Do not waste even a minute of your human life.' Use every opportunity for your eternal welfare. A sweet story illustrates the above verse:

Once a fisherman left his home with his fishing net before dawn. He reached the stream, decided to wait until there was sufficient light and then cast his net into the river. He sat down upon a boulder on the river bank. His feet were in the water while he relished the pre-dawn quietude.

The fisherman then realised that there was a bundle on the river bed, under his feet. Lazily, he picked it up and put his hand in. It seemed to contain some hard, round objects. He thought they were probably pebbles. He casually took out one pebble and tossed it into the river. There was a plop as it fell into the water.

The sound was pleasing to the ear. The fisherman took out another pebble and chucked it casually into the water. It became like a game and was a good way to pass time while he sat on the river bank. In this manner, he threw twenty-four pebbles from the cloth bag into the river.

Finally, the last pebble was in his hand. By now, there was sufficient light for him to see. He cast a glance at what was in his hand and was shocked to discover that it was a priceless jewel. He rued his actions. 'God gave me twenty-five such precious gems, and in my ignorance, I threw away twenty-four of them. How unfortunate I am!' he cried.

In the above story, the fisherman at least got one jewel for himself. But if we are not cautious, we will be even more unfortunate. More valuable than the precious stones is a gift that God has given us all—the gift of the human form. In our ignorance, we are wasting it away in frivolous activities. The Ramayan states:

nara tanu pāī visaya man dehī
  palaṭi sudhā te saṭha visa lāhī
tāhiṅ kabahuñ bhala kahai na koī
  guñjā grahai parasa maṇi khoī
ākara chāri lachchha chaurāsī
  joni bhramata yaha jīva avināsī
phirata sadā māyā kara prerā
  kāla karma subhava guna gherā

'O humans! You have received this rare birth and are wasting it in sensual gratification. It is like giving away nectar and taking poison in return. How can you be considered intelligent when you are exchanging *paras* (philosopher's stone) for broken pieces of glass? Consequently, you will keep rotating within the 8.4 million species of life. And even though you are the eternal soul, you will remain in material bondage, tied to the three guṇas and the stockpile of your past karmas.'

Let us then contemplate upon this knowledge to fill ourselves with enthusiasm. In this chapter, we have seen how inspiration is the fuel that propels us to produce the winning edge in our work. It changes the way we look at things and enriches our life experiences. It is the sword that enables us to cut through difficulties, and the anchor that brings us to victory from the brink of defeat. We have also discussed how to become internally motivated by the proper use of the intellect.

And yet, even inspiration is not sufficient. Thieves, murderers and terrorists are also inspired, but what they lack is a proper purpose. Thus, let us now move on to the fourth mindset for success, which is 'purity of intention'.

CHAPTER 4

THE MINDSET OF PURITY OF INTENTION

In the last chapter, we discussed the importance of enthusiasm, the power source within us with the potential energy to propel us to tremendous action. However, mere energy is not enough; it must also be focussed in the right direction. The infamous criminal, Al Capone, was highly motivated, and so was the notorious Indian dacoit, Veerappan. Unfortunately, their zeal was misdirected and harmful. Enthusiasm without proper direction is like a high-speed car with broken steering and no brakes. Thus, having discussed inspiration, the next essential ingredient needed for success that we shall talk about is 'purity of intention'.

Let us start the discussion with a case of impure intention:

A few years ago, the Satyam scam shook the Indian corporate world. It was perhaps the biggest corporate fraud to come to light in India. Satyam Computers had been at the forefront of India's IT revolution for many years. Its chairman, Ramalinga Raju, was found to have swindled the company of over ten thousand crore rupees (1.3 billion dollars). A high-power enquiry revealed that for years, he had been siphoning off funds by fraudulent means such as non-existent employees on company rolls, loans to kith and kin, insider trading and improper acquisitions. With the amassed wealth, he had purchased villas and properties in sixty countries. Sixteen luxury cars and three hundred pairs of shoes were found in his possession. The fraud shook the corporate world in 2009, leading to the collapse of Satyam Computers. Ramalinga Raju was finally convicted in 2015.

Ramalinga Raju undoubtedly had talent and intelligence. He did his MBA from Ohio and was enrolled in the Owner/President Management programme at Harvard Business School. His ace management skills, foresight and immense desire to succeed propelled Satyam to the vanguard of information technology worldwide. What he lacked was the purity of intention. He mis-utilised his God-given talents, connections and resources for self-aggrandisement and puny gratification, thereby cheating the shareholders, employees and investors who had trusted him.

Ramalinga Raju's case was an extreme example of impure intention. But what if he had not done anything illegal and merely used his talents to chase worldly pleasures and a legally comfortable life? Would that still be labelled as impure intention? When is intention considered impure? How does impure intention harm us? Let us find out the answers to these questions in a step-by-step manner.

If Ramalinga Raju were to be asked about the intent behind such a fraud, he would have probably answered that he was pursuing success. Or he may have said that he was protecting the success he had already achieved. Success, for him, meant financial abundance, corporate dominance and societal prestige. Could we then fault his intention? His intention, very clearly, was to succeed in life. The problem was that his definition of success itself was warped, and that was the reason behind his downfall.

Our intention will be considered pure when our definition of success is pure, and we are sincerely striving to achieve it. Therefore, to understand the nature of pure intention, we first need to discuss the definition of true success.

What Is Success in Life?

We all wish to make our life a success. Nobody desires to fail except those suffering from psychological imbalance. Thus, the universal intention of humankind is to succeed. The problem is that if our concept of success is wrong, then our efforts will also be misdirected. How, then, should we correctly define success?

Many people believe they would consider themselves successful only if they could become billionaires, for then they would possess their own limousine, private plane, personal boat and palatial house. But if financial prosperity is the measure of success, then shouldn't multi-millionaires be the happiest people in the world? However, if you were to conduct an enquiry into the lives of the super-rich, you would find the reality to be the exact opposite. Several multi-millionaires cannot sleep unless they take sleeping pills. Howard Hughes, an American businessman and film director, was a prime example. He was one of the wealthiest people in the world in his time. Yet, he died in mental misery, secluding himself from society due to bouts of depression and paranoia. The truth is that people may possess all the wealth in the world, but if their mind is agitated, they can never be happy.

Some people claim that if only they could become famous worldwide, their life would undoubtedly be a success. They associate accomplishment and triumph in life with the accumulation of a huge amount of fame. However, there are innumerable examples of immensely famous people who were so miserable from inside that they committed suicide. Take the case of the King of Rock 'n' Roll, Elvis Presley. The American singer, actor and cultural icon of a generation was also the most-celebrated solo artist in the entire history of recorded albums. The sale of his albums almost touched one billion. And yet, he struggled with depression and died at a young age from a drug overdose.

Another section of people tie their success to the attainment of powerful titles. They are desperate for high positions. In their value system, an MLA is reasonably successful, an MP is definitely successful, a chief minister is greatly successful, and a prime minister is super-duper successful. But they do not realise that no matter what position one attains, the mind starts yearning to reach the next level. The MLA is unhappy because he wants to become an MP; the MP is discontented because he yearns to be a chief minister; the chief minister longs for the position of the prime minister; and the prime minister is worried about how to get re-elected. Hence, despite the status we occupy, happiness remains as elusive as a mirage in the desert.

Obviously, mere financial wealth, social popularity and powerful positions are not the correct parameters for success. Besides, where do peace and joy figure in the above definitions of accomplished living? Success can never satisfy a person if it does not bestow peace of mind.

Joshua Liebman, an American Jewish rabbi, relates a beautiful tale in his book, Peace of Mind. *He describes that as a teenager, he made a list of all that he should aspire for in his life. He then took this list to a wise person in his neighbourhood. The astute old neighbour looked at Joshua's list and said, 'Young man, the list is thoughtfully framed. But one item is missing. And without it, all else is useless.'*

'What is this item that is so critical?' enquired Joshua.

'Peace of mind,' replied the astute neighbour. 'If you do not have peace, you will be miserable and unhappy. What will be the use of all other attainments?'

Joshua's neighbour wisely pointed out that any definition of accomplishment in life that does not include peace is shallow and incomplete. What, then, is the proper and complete meaning of success?

The Oxford Dictionary gives two primary definitions of success: 1) attainment of fame, wealth or status, and 2) achievement of an aim or purpose. The first definition is way off the mark, as we have seen in the previously mentioned examples of wealthy, powerful and famous people.

Let us now turn to some famous writers and thinkers to see how they defined success.

- Deepak Chopra, famous writer and wellness coach, writes, 'Success in life could be defined as the continued expansion of happiness and the progressive realisation of worthy goals.'
- Warren Buffet, entrepreneur and business tycoon, says, 'I measure success by how many people love me.'
- Self-help writer, Stephen Covey, looked on success as deeply individual. 'If you carefully consider what you want to be said of you in the funeral experience, you will find your definition of success.'
- Winston Churchill stated, 'Success is going from failure to failure without losing enthusiasm.'
- Billionaire Richard Branson says, 'The more you are actively and practically engaged, the more successful you will feel.'

All the above definitions help us get whiffs of the meaning of success, but they do not present a comprehensive concept of it. Nor does the internet offer a reasonable definition. Based upon the Vedic scriptures, I have outlined below a more comprehensive understanding of successful living.

We all have three common yearnings: 1) to be good, 2) to do good and 3) to feel good. Accordingly, success in life should be measured against these three criteria:

1) To become the best we can be
2) To do the best we can in the works we undertake
3) To experience happiness and satisfaction in life

Let us look at these three points in detail.

To Become the Best We Can Be

Why do we all have the urge to be good? The reason is that our soul is by nature divine and an eternal part of God. Thus, we all naturally love divine virtues such as compassion, justice, authenticity and truthfulness. Unholy qualities like deceit, cruelty, falsehood and hypocrisy go against our intrinsic soulful nature. Hence, we always expect others to behave with us in a just and righteous manner.

Some people contest the above statement and say, 'How can you claim that everyone loves divine qualities? There are so many in the world who swear by falsehood and deceit.'

Well, I did not imply that nobody in the world is unrighteous and untruthful. But if you behave unjustly with those who deceive you, will they like it? Definitely not! They will object big time. Consider the following conversation:

'Why did you lie to me?'

'Well, you tell lies yourself. If I told you a lie, why is it a big deal?'

'Never mind if I tell lies, but I do not want anyone to lie to me.'

This is called honesty amongst thieves. Even the leader of a gang of robbers expects the gang members to be truthful to him.

In other words, irrespective of our behaviour and attitude, we *always* expect justice and compassion from others. A story from the Mahabharat reveals this nicely:

When Karn's chariot wheel became stuck in the ground, he got down and began to dislodge it. At that time, Lord Krishna instructed Arjun, 'Shoot him in the back. When his chest is towards you, it will not be possible for you to kill him.'

Karn heard Shree Krishna's words. He responded, 'O Krishna, You are the Supreme Lord, and You are teaching deceit to Arjun. You manifested the Vedas, in which You revealed the dharma for warriors—one should not shoot after sunset, one should not shoot below the belt and one should not shoot the enemy in the back. Yet, today, You are teaching adharma to Arjun?

kṣhatra dharmamavekṣhasva

'O Shree Krishna, what is the dharma of warriors? Think, think.'

Lord Krishna replied:

kva dharmaste tadā gataḥ

'O Karn, what dharma did you follow at that time?'

If Karn loved dharma so much, then why did he fight on the side of the unrighteous Kauravas in this war? Where did his dharma go when Draupadi was being humiliated? And where did his dharma go when the Kauravas were usurping the rightful share of the Pandavas? He was siding with the unholy Kauravas, and yet expecting righteous behaviour from the Pandavas.

The story illustrates how even those who cheat others do not wish anyone else to cheat them. We always expect righteous conduct from others. Here is another illustration of the same principle:

A thief stole from someone's house and returned to his home. He was pleased. 'I have grabbed a large treasure today,' he said to himself. Having counted his booty, he went to sleep.

At night, another burglar entered his home and plundered it. When the first thief woke up, he was furious. 'Who did this? Does he not know who I am? If I find him, I will finish him.'

Now, if we ask the first thief, 'Why are you so agitated? You are a burglar yourself. If someone stole from you, it should delight you that earlier there was only one thief in this subdivision, and now there are two. Your party has doubled!'

The first thief will respond, 'No, I have the right to rob from others. But nobody should steal from me.'

We always expect behaviour that is kind, just and honest from others. These are godly virtues, and since we are little children of God, we all instinctively love these virtues. We all seek to overcome our flaws and develop divine qualities.

Hence, the desire to grow in virtue, and become the best person we can be, is a universal common desire. Accordingly, the first criteria for success in life is to be good, virtuous and pure.

It needs to be mentioned here that nobody transforms from a sinner to a saint in a day. The process of growth is always gradual and incremental. The important thing then is to see whether we are putting in our best efforts to grow. We can take inspiration regarding this from Edmund Hillary.

We all know that in 1953, Edmund Hillary and Sherpa Tenzing became the first people to climb Mount Everest, the highest mountain in the world. It was a feat that required utmost courage, determination and physical endurance. However, few people are aware that both Hillary and Tenzing had separately attempted to scale the same mountain earlier, but had failed.

An association of mountaineers in England came to know of Hillary's 1951 attempt on Everest and organised a programme to felicitate him. Before the assembled gathering of mountaineers, Hillary was invited to the stage to speak. There was a picture of Everest on the stage.

Edmund Hillary walked up to the picture, and shaking his fist before it, said, 'Everest, you defeated me this time. But next time, I will defeat you. Because you have grown to your maximum potential, while I am still growing.'

The urge to keep growing is the intrinsic nature of our soul. It will never be satiated until we reach the ultimate state of God-realisation. Along these lines, Swami Vivekananda stated:

These Prophets were not unique; they were men as you and I. They had attained superconsciousness, and you and I can do the same. The very fact that one person attained that state indicates that all men can do so. And that, ultimately, is religion.

In the same manner, the Bible states:

Be perfect, therefore, as your heavenly Father is perfect.

(Matthew 5:48)

The purpose of religion is to help us become godlike in virtue and goodness. Of course, that can only happen by the grace of God, but He is ever-eager to bestow that grace upon us. That is why a name for God in the Vedas is Brahman. Jagadguru Shree Kripalu-ji Maharaj explained the meaning of Brahman in the following manner:

brahma vṛihatvāt asa baṛā jāko ādi na anta
baṛā bṛinhaṇatvāt asa aurana kare ananta

(*Bhakti Śhatak* verse 51)

The verse states that the word 'Brahman' has two meanings. The first meaning is 'He who is infinitely big—without beginning or end.' The second meaning is 'He who makes others infinitely big—like Himself.' In other words, God is not miserly to withhold greatness from the souls. Rather, He wants them, His little parts, to grow in divine virtues and become perfect, like Himself.

Thus, the goal of the human journey is to keep growing in virtue. Of course, nobody can be perfect without completing the journey. But if we are trying to be the best we can presently be, then we are leading a successful life.

Now, let us discuss the second aspect of success.

To Do the Best in the Work We Undertake

The yearning of our soul does not end with the desire to be good. We also seek to be productive. We wish to see our talents utilised meaningfully as the below story illustrates.

There was once a woodcutter who worked at a timber farm in Karnataka, on hourly wages. A researcher of behavioural psychology approached him and offered him a job on his farm at double the wage. Next day, the brawny woodcutter reported to the researcher's farm. 'What do I need to do?' he asked the psychologist.

'Take this axe and hit it on that tree there, for eight hours every day. I do not want you to cut it. I only need you to hit the tree with the back of your axe head, not the sharp edge.'

'Really? What use will that be? It will never get cut, and I will be hitting the same tree day in and day out, all the months of the year.'

'Why should it matter to you? You will be receiving double the salary. Simply do what you are being asked.'

Inspired by his doubled pay package, the woodcutter went to work. He would hit the tree with the back of the axe head about five hundred times every hour from morning to night. Naturally, his blows neither cut the tree nor chipped the wood. But he did not care as he was receiving the money for his efforts.

But after a few days, he became bored. On the tenth day, he took his axe to the researcher and said, 'I quit. Here is your axe.'

'Why are you quitting this job? Is it not lucrative for you?'

'It is lucrative, but it is no fun. I need to see the chips flying to feel that I am doing something worthwhile.'

That is the reality of human nature. We all want to see the chips flying in the different works we do. Of course, we all perform different tasks. We are all blessed with different talents, for that is the variety inherent in creation.

In nature, we see the hummingbird that weighs only one-tenth of an ounce. It has hollow bones to ensure its featherlight weight. It is the lightest of all birds. We also see the ostrich that weighs about three hundred pounds, making it the heaviest of all birds. Interestingly, both these birds have their own speciality.

The hummingbird flaps its wings seventy-five times a second, allowing it to hover at a single spot in the air while it sucks nectar from flowers. Its light weight makes this possible. On the other hand, the ostrich cannot fly because of its heaviness. Yet, it hops long distances on the ground, enabling it to run at a speed of eighty kilometres an hour, which is faster than even world champion sprinters. Likewise, every creature in nature has been endowed with its own unique specialities.

We humans too are all different. Each of us is uniquely gifted with our individual talents. One may be brilliant enough to be the president of a country, while another may be a talented and exceptional clerk in an office. Yet, both wish to see their innate abilities productively utilised to make a difference in the world. Both desire to see themselves beneficially impacting the lives of people around them. Thus, the second criteria for a successful life is to do the best we can in the work we undertake.

Let us now come to the third dimension of success.

To Experience Happiness and Satisfaction in Life

Ultimately, life is all about attaining happiness. We all want to be happy. Everything else we seek is only an intermediate goal. For example, one yearns for a good job, another pines for a beautiful spouse, and the third intensely desires a palatial home. It may seem that they have different desires, but each of these yearnings is in the pursuit of happiness. Thus, the search for happiness is our common goal, and twenty-four hours a day, all our activities are directed towards reaching it.

This principle was well understood by Aristotle, the wise man from Greece. Hence, he said twenty-five hundred years ago:

> We choose honour, wealth and prestige because they bring us happiness. But we choose happiness for itself and never with a view for anything further.

Amazingly, twenty-five hundred years before Aristotle, Sage Ved Vyas had already stated:

> *sarveṣhām api bhūtānāṁ nṛipa svātmaiva vallabhaḥ*
> *itare 'patya-vittādyās tad-vallabhatayaiva hi*
> (Shreemad Bhagavatam 10.14.50)

'Everyone loves their happiness. It is only for the sake of self-happiness that they love child, wealth, etc.'

Now, consider this question: Did anybody teach us to seek happiness, just as we had to learn everything else? As children, we were taught: 'My child, you should always speak the truth', 'Son, you should obey and respect your elders', 'My daughter, you should never steal from anyone', etc. But we were not coached, 'You must always seek happiness. It should not come to a point that you start searching for misery.' This instruction was never given to us. It means that without ever being taught, we intuitively decided that bliss is what we want.

In fact, the moment we were born, the first thing we did was to express, 'I have come into the world, and I want happiness.' We did not say it in words since we could not speak, but we cried with all our might. Why did we cry upon birth? It was because during the process of birth, we experienced pain, and we sobbed to reveal our nature. 'I have not come to the earth for pain. I have come for bliss. Give me pleasure, not misery!'

Since then, until this day, all we have done is in the pursuit of happiness. In light of this, we can safely conclude that the goal of all living beings is happiness.

Why do we all desire happiness? The answer to this question is found in the Vedic scriptures. They declare that we are all looking for bliss because God is an ocean of bliss.

ānando brahmeti vyajānāt (*Taittirīya Upaniṣhad* 3.6)

ānandamayo 'bhyāsāt (*Vedānt Darśhan* 1.1.12)

ānanda sindhu madhya tava vāsā (Ramayan)

Anand means bliss. The above verses from the Vedic scriptures state that God is an ocean of infinite happiness. We souls are tiny parts of God, hence we all are little fragments of the ocean of bliss.

Every part is naturally attracted to its source. A lump of mud is a part of the earth and is drawn towards it. If you throw it up, it will fall, pulled by the gravitational force of the earth. That is how Newton discovered gravitational force, when an apple fell on his head. In the same way, our soul is a tiny fragment of the ocean of bliss and naturally yearns for happiness.

Thus, the urge to feel good is also universal. Material pleasures, no matter how attractive they may seem, are unable to satisfy this longing, since it is for the infinite bliss of God.

Only when we purify our mind do we get the happiness that is truly satisfying. The happiness we are searching for is not on the outside; rather, it is within us and is accessed through purity.

The Ramayan states: *nirmala mana jana so mohi pāvā.* 'The pure at heart are the ones who attain Me.'

Similarly, the Bible states: 'Blessed are the pure in heart, for they will see God.'   (Matthew 5:8)

In conclusion, a successful life requires the satisfaction of three points:

1)   To become the best we can be
2)   To do the best we can in the work we undertake
3)   To experience happiness and satisfaction in life

All these three points can be summarised in the following manner: **Success in life means to be good, to do good and to feel good.**

Having understood a deeper meaning of success, let us now get a grip on the subject of pure versus impure intention.

What Is Pure Intention?

People have a variety of reasons for their actions. The intention could be self-glorification and gratification of the ego, it could be envy and the desire to put others down or it could be the craving to satiate the yearnings of the senses. Noble values motivate some, others are inspired by faith in the divine knowledge of the scriptures, and so on. The variety of possible intentions is an endless spectrum as the story below illustrates.

A temple was being constructed in the holy city of Vrindavan, and workers were carrying trays of brick on the site. A sage asked the first worker, 'What are you doing?'

He retorted, 'Can you not see? I am carrying a load of bricks.'

The second worker was asked what he was doing. He answered, 'I am earning a living for my family.'

The third worker was queried on his work. He replied, 'I am building a temple for Lord Krishna.'

Although they were doing the same job, their attitudes were so different.

According to Vedic literature, there are four categories of people and their corresponding intentions:

1) **Tāmasic people (in the mode of ignorance):** They cheat, swindle and rob others to fulfil their needs. They do not care for the rules of God, scriptures or society. If something suits them, they feel justified in doing it; and it matters little that it could be harmful to others. The intention of Ramalinga Raju, as discussed above, falls in this category.

2) **Rājasic people (in the mode of passion):** They earn money legally and use it for their pleasure and needs. Rājasic people do not break the law, but are driven by materialistic desires for the gratification of their mind and senses. Even if they engage in social welfare, the primary motive is the prestige it brings them. They donate in charity to gain name and fame in society. Rājasic people justifiably look down upon tāmasic people as cheats and violators of the law, but they do not realise that they

are transgressing the divine law, as will be explained subsequently.

3) **Sāttvic people (in the mode of goodness):** They are driven by higher virtues like compassion and generosity. They take part in service projects for others and society at large. Honest social workers, philanthropists, knowledge seekers and researchers belong to this category. The intention of sāttvic people is purer and more selfless compared to rājasic people. However, in the light of divine knowledge, it is still impure, because it is devoid of God-consciousness.

4) *Guṇātīt* **people (beyond the three modes of material nature):** They are established in their loving relationship with God. Every work of theirs is inspired by love for the divine, and consequently, the intention behind every action of theirs is to please Him. Such an intention is truly pure.

Understand this through the example of a human hand. It is an integral part of the body, and its natural function is to serve the body. The hand lifts food from the plate and puts it in the mouth; it carries the tumbler of water and brings it to the lips; it holds the toothbrush and cleans the teeth with it. In this manner, day and night, the hand serves the aggregate physical personality. Now, suppose the hand was to get tired of serving, and plead, 'Service, service, service ... I have had enough. Sever me from the body; I will take care of myself.'

Severed from the body, can the hand cater to its needs? No. Without its connection to the body, it will remain a mere lump of flesh. The self-interest of the hand is in serving the body.

By doing so, it automatically receives the blood, nutrition and oxygen required for its survival. In other words, the hand does not have to fend for itself. Its dharma is to serve the body, of which it is an integral part.

In the same manner, we souls too are tiny fragments of God. Like the severed hand, we have turned our consciousness away from our Source. In this disconnected state, we say, 'Why should I serve God? I will find my bliss independent of Him.' This is material consciousness—where the soul has its face away from God. In this state of forgetfulness, we have been wandering in the cycle of life and death since innumerable lifetimes and have neither found true love, nor true knowledge, nor true happiness.

When we reconnect ourselves with our Source, we begin to do our every work for His pleasure. And only then does our soul experience the bliss it has been searching for since endless lifetimes. Thus, **purity of intention is the desire to please God with our every thought, word and deed.** The Bhagavad Gita states the same principle:

yat karoṣhi yad aśhnāsi yaj juhoṣhi dadāsi yat
yat tapasyasi kaunteya tat kuruṣhva mad-arpaṇam (9.27)

Lord Krishna said to Arjun: 'Whatever you do, whatever you eat, whatever sacrifices you perform, whatever you give away in charity and whatever austerities you undertake, do them all as an offering unto Me.'

Taking this theme forward, here is an inspiring story told of Chhatrapati Shivaji, the Maratha warrior king:

Shivaji's guru was a renunciant monk called Samarth Ramdas. Once Shivaji was standing on the terrace of his palace when he saw his guru enter the street in front. Samarth Ramdas had a begging bowl in his hand and was asking for alms from onlookers and passersby, 'Bhikshām dehī ... Bhikshām dehī ...'

Shivaji felt extremely embarrassed. He thought, 'I am the king of the land, and my guru is begging for alms. This is very shameful for me.'

Suddenly, a noble thought crossed Shivaji's mind. He wrote something on a piece of paper and ran down the palace stairs. He reached Samarth Ramdas and put the slip of paper in his guru's begging bowl.

Gurudev opened the slip and read it. Shivaji had written, 'I donate my kingdom and everything in it to you.'

Samarth Ramdas smiled. He said, 'My child, this is a beautiful gesture of surrender from your side. But I am an ascetic monk. I beg for alms not because I have a need, but because it gives me the opportunity to meet people in household life, share words of wisdom with them and provide them with opportunities to serve a sadhu. What will I do with your kingdom? I am giving it back to you. But remember that henceforth, the kingdom is not yours; it belongs to your guru, and you are only his representative. Rule it on my behalf, doing everything as a service to God and guru.'

Samarth Ramdas had given his royal disciple the best lesson in purity of intention. Shivaji continued to rule his kingdom, but his consciousness changed. Earlier, he was doing it for his sake, and now he began performing the same duties as a service to God.

Our Soul Notifies Us When the Intention Is Impure

People often ask the question: 'How can I know if my intention is pure?'

The answer is that our soul intimates us of it. When our intention is impure, the soul does not experience the divine bliss of God. Our experience tells us, 'I am not truly happy.' Conversely, on acting with pure intention, we get divine bliss from within, and our feeling tells us, 'I am experiencing inner joy.'

For example, how do we know that we are hungry? There is no external proof for it. Our senses inform us that we are hungry. Similarly, when we have eaten, how do we know that we are full? Again, our stomach feels full and tells us that the appetite is satiated.

Likewise, our experience informs us when we receive the divine bliss of God. Sage Narad was asked, 'What is the proof of bhakti?' He responded:

pramāṇāntarasyānapekṣhatvāt svayaṁ pramāṇatvāt
(*Nārad Bhakti Darśhan* Sutra 59)

'Bhakti does not require any external proof. When you engage in true bhakti, your own experience of inner satisfaction gives you the proof.' There are days when you sit for devotion in front of your altar, but the mind is unable to focus due to anxiety, desire, etc. At that time, your inner feeling informs you that something is missing, and you are not satisfied. And on other days, when your mind is imbued with noble thoughts and lovingly absorbed in God, you get the deep satisfaction of the soul. Your experience apprises you that your devotion went well.

This can also be compared to a game of tennis or cricket. In cricket, when you hit a well-timed stroke with your bat, you do not need to see where the ball went. Your feeling lets you know that it was a perfect shot and the ball will probably cross the boundary. Similarly, when the shot is not executed properly, you do not get the satisfaction of playing a good shot. Without even looking at where the ball went, you realise that the stroke left much to be desired.

Likewise, the satisfaction that our soul is seeking comes from purity of intention, purity of effort and purity of feelings. If there is impurity, our inner sense of dissatisfaction conveys to us that there is yet much to be desired.

You may be astonished to know that even gross negative feelings—tension, anxiety, unhappiness, stress, etc.—are consequences of impure intention. Let us learn how.

The Modern-Day Epidemic of Stress

In present times, stress management has become a big concern. But what exactly is 'stress'? An engineer would define it as the force in a machine part, a beam or a structure that tends to break, shear, twist or crush it. Similarly, we humans too experience stress in our emotional personality when we interact with the external world. Psychologists have concluded that when we perceive that the situation at hand requires more financial, spiritual, physical or intellectual resources than we possess, we feel stressed.

As children, when we were unprepared for our annual, year-end exam scheduled for the next day, we experienced stress.

Now, as adults, we perceive stress when the manager tells us that our work performance has been unsatisfactory, and our job is in danger. The situations of stress can be innumerable and variegated.

What happens to our mind and body in the face of stress? In 1915, the Harvard psychologist, Walter Cannon, observed the 'fight-or-flight response'. He found that when animals are faced with a stressful situation where their life is endangered, their body responds in a manner that enhances their chances of survival. Their heart pounds more rapidly thereby pumping more blood. Blood flow is diverted from the skin to the muscles, so that in the case of a tear, blood loss will be reduced. Sweat glands function overtime to cool the muscles. And the mind becomes riveted on the object of the threat. All this enables the animal to do one of two things—either fight the danger at hand, or, if the attacker is more powerful, then take flight. This is the natural instinct of animals to sustain their existence.

It has been well established that the human body mechanism too undergoes the same physical and mental 'fight-or-flight response' in the face of danger. Adrenaline gets pumped into the blood making the heart race. Blood pressure increases and the body breaks into a sweat. Now, in the 21st century, the dangers we face are invariably not to life. They could be financial pressures, social affronts or emotional conflicts. All these require a composed mind and a calm body to handle them best. It does not help if our heart is pounding away. Unfortunately, the human mechanism responds to perceived threats with the same 'fight-or-flight response' as in animals.

Instead of thinking logically, the mind becomes obsessed with the threat. And none of this helps to handle the situation.

Further, stress has an impact on our health. Regular functions of the immune system are altered, and the digestive system is suppressed. In modern society, a stressful situation does not stay for a few moments. It remains for days and even months, in the form of deadlines to be met, mortgage payments to be made, etc. The consequential continued activation of the stress-response system results in an excessive release of cortisol and other stress hormones, which disrupt the normal bodily processes. This increases the risk of several health problems such as depression, indigestion, headaches, heart ailment, sleep loss, weight gain, memory impairment, etc. Hence the need for stress management.

The Root Cause of Stress

What is the primary reason for the stress we experience? Nobody seems to know the answer to this. If you search the internet for the causes of stress, search engines come up with all kinds of superficial reasons. The popular medical website, *WebMD*, lists the following causes for stress:

- Being unhappy at your job
- Having a heavy workload or too much responsibility
- Working long hours
- Having no say in the decision-making process
- Being insecure about your chance for advancement
- Risk of termination

- Having to give speeches in front of colleagues
- Facing discrimination or harassment at work

Other websites on stress management also provide similar external causes for stress. However, they all fail to identify the root cause. And since people do not understand why it arises, all the so-called solutions they propound for stress are merely symptomatic, such as yoga, tai chi, meditation, listening to calming music, time management, situation management, etc.

This can be compared to having a high fever due to malaria. If one takes paracetamol, the symptom will be suppressed—the fever will decrease—but the disease will not be cured. In the same way, doing yoga, meditation, tai chi, etc. are merely symptomatic cures for stress, but none of these techniques address the root of the problem. Then, what is the cause for stress within us?

Stress develops when we are attached to a particular outcome and are worried that things may not turn out as we desire. For example, if a businessperson is attached to making profits but fears incurring a loss, it results in stress. If a sales representative wishes to meet a particular sales target but is apprehensive of doing so, the condition of stress ensues. It means that the reason for stress is our attachment to a particular outcome, and our unwillingness to accept other possible outcomes.

This point needs to be understood in depth. Stress is not caused by hard work. Often we feel that our arduous effort is stressing us out. But that is an incorrect understanding. You can be working from morning to night and still not be tense.

One student came to me and said, 'Swami-ji, I have an important exam in three months, and it is stressing me out.'

I asked him, 'Are you experiencing tension because of the intense study that you are doing?'

He responded, 'Yes.'

'Think again.' I explained to him, 'It is not the studies per se that are the cause of your anxiety. You are attached to a particular outcome. And that is what is harassing you. When your school arranges for an internal assessment to help you prepare, you study equally hard for it, but do not feel any tension. That is because you know the outcome is of no consequence. But in the case of the external exam, you have become emotionally invested in the outcome, which is the cause of your stress.'

People often ask me, 'Swami-ji, you work fifteen hours a day, for 365 days a year. You interact with thousands of people and manage scores of congregational centres and dozens of ashrams. Yet, we never see you harried.' Well, the reason is, that while working hard and trying my best, I leave the results in the hands of God. Since I am not attached to outcomes, it enables me to stay stress-free.

In conclusion, what stresses us is not hard work but attachment to the results.

The Remedy for Stress

Once we understand the cause of stress, the remedy is simple—give up attachment to the outcome. Simply focus on your efforts, not on the results. This science of work was explained in the Bhagavad Gita five thousand years ago:

karmaṇy evādhikāras te mā phaleṣhu kadāchana   (2.47)

Lord Krishna tells Arjun: 'You have a right to perform your work, but you are not entitled to the fruits.' Relish your work and offer its fruits to God.

The outcome of our efforts is not in our hands in any case. It depends upon several factors such as circumstances, assistance from others, efforts of competitors, sheer luck, coincidence and the will of God. Thus, wisdom demands that having put in our best, we should be content with whatever results we get. There have been many inspiring Indian leaders who practised the Bhagavad Gita's science of work.

Bal Gangadhar Tilak, a leader of the Indian freedom struggle before Mahatma Gandhi, was reputed as a karm yogi. His mindset towards his work exemplified detachment from the fruit of his labour. Once, the British police came to his home to arrest him under Section 124 of the law. He asked them to wait for five minutes. He then told his friend to contact an attorney to find out what his rights were under Section 124, and then come to the jail and inform him about the same. Tilak then allowed the policemen to take him to the jail, where he immediately went to sleep without a worrisome thought. When his friend arrived at the jail, he found Tilak sleeping like a child. He was merely focussed on doing his best for the cause he was dedicated to, but was detached from the outcome.

In another incident, Tilak was working in his office when a clerk came to him from his residence. He said, 'Your elder son is extremely unwell.' Tilak asked the clerk to get a doctor to see him.

Half an hour later, a friend came and said, 'Your son is unwell, and you are not worried?'

Tilak replied, 'How will worrying help me? I have asked the doctor to see him. What else can I do?'

Another time, he was asked what he would like to become if India got independence—foreign minister or prime minister. He responded, 'My ambition was to write a book on differential calculus. I will fulfil it.' He was leading a national movement, and yet he was so detached.

We can see how Tilak was at great peace with himself and his work, even though he was leading a nationwide movement against the colonial government. The secret was his attitude of merely focussing upon doing his best and leaving the rest to God.

Some people raise a doubt here: 'If we are not attached to results, will it not impact our performance? Will we not lapse in our professional competence?'

On the contrary, nothing could be further from the truth. When we are free from debilitating emotions such as tension, anxiety and nervousness, our effectiveness will only increase. For example, most business people know that if they become anxious during negotiations, they are liable to commit mistakes. 'Keep your cool,' as they say, is an implied reference to detachment from the outcome.

If we keep worrying about what the outcome will be, the mind becomes divided, and it distracts us from the work at hand. Instead, when we focus upon our efforts, it automatically helps us get the best possible outcome.

Let us now proceed further. How can we give up attachment to the outcome of our efforts? For this, we need to learn the practice of karm yog.

Karm Yog—The Art of Working in Divine Consciousness

Karm yog literally means 'karm' plus 'yog'. To understand it, we first need to appreciate the true meaning of yog. Nowadays, yoga has become a buzzword in the western world. Yoga studios have mushroomed in every major city of the developed world. Recent studies reveal that in the US, thirty-two million people practise yoga, which is about one out of ten. And an equal number say that they are likely to begin in the near future.

It is very heartening to see India's ancient science become so popular. However, most yoga practitioners have adopted it for good health, as a beauty aid or for weight loss. That is all very well, but they are unaware of the spiritual depth of the 'science of yog'. The postures of yog are called asanas. Asanas are only the third limb of the eight-fold system called *Aṣhṭāṅg Yog*, which has seven more limbs. The entire sequence is:

yama-niyamāsana-prāṇāyāma-pratyāhāra-dhāraṇā-
dhyāna-samādhayo' ṣhṭāvaṅgāni
(Patañjali Yog Darśhan 2.29)

The eight limbs of yog are *yam* (abstinence), *niyam* (codes of conduct), *āsan* (postures), *prāṇāyām* (breath control), *pratyāhār* (turning inward), *dhāraṇā* (concentration), *dhyān* (meditation) and *samādhi* (complete absorption in God).

The limbs of the system help us prepare for yog. The word 'yog' means 'union'. For example, in ayurveda, when two medicines are combined, it is called yog. In the spiritual context, yog refers to the linking of the individual soul with the Supreme Soul. Thus, the ultimate goal of the yogic system is to connect with God.

> *sanyogo yoga ityukto jīvātmā paramātmanoḥ*
>
> (*Garuḍ Purāṇ*)

'The union of the individual consciousness with the Supreme Consciousness is yog.' This linking takes place when the mind is absorbed in loving remembrance of God.

When we are able to keep the mind in divine consciousness and continue doing our worldly duties alongside, that is 'karm yog'. There have been many karm yogis in Indian history. Dhruv, Prahlad, Ambarish, Prithu, Yudhishthir, etc. were all great emperors. As sovereigns, they were constantly surrounded by people and had to fulfil many complex tasks for the administration of their kingdom, yet, internally, their consciousness was always absorbed in the Lord. Saint Kabir, who was himself a karm yogi in household life, said:

> *jahañ jahañ chalūñ karūñ parikramā, jo jo karūñ so pūjā*
> *jaba soūñ karūñ daṇḍavat, jānūñ deva na dūjā*

'Whenever I walk, I think I am doing parikramā (circumambulation) of the Lord. Whatever work I do, I offer it to Him. When I sleep, I think I am paying prostrate obeisance. In this way, I worship my Lord with my every action, and I do not know anyone apart from Him.'

Most people have separated puja from their daily lives. They engage in devotion for a little while in their puja room. But when they emerge from it, they forget about God. They go about their daily chores with an impure mind immersed in desire, attachment, greed, pride and anxiety.

The practice of karm yog changes that. We keep our mind attached to God, no matter where we go and what we do. Then, every work we perform becomes an offering to Him. Thus, in karm yog, we do not divide our activities, thinking 'this work is for me and this is for my Lord'. Instead, since the mind is always absorbed in God, every action becomes an offering at the altar of the Supreme. When every work of ours becomes worship of the Lord, then automatically our intention rises above tāmasic, rājasic and sāttvic states, and becomes guṇātīt (divinely pure).

Let us take a look at how we can transform all our material duties into service for the Lord and thereby purify our intention. Consider, for example, that we have to earn money to maintain ourselves—the activity of earning money is considered material work. But the same can be spiritualised by thinking in this manner: 'My family members are all children of God, and He has entrusted them to my care. Let me earn well so that I can take care of them, and whatever I can save, I will serve God and guru with it.' In this way, earning money through one's profession becomes divine service.

Similarly, eating is one activity we all have to do—it is also material work. We can make it an offering for the pleasure of God, by thinking: 'This body is the vehicle with which I serve God. It must remain strong, so that I can engage in bhakti with it. As a result, let me eat healthy food to take good care of my body.'

Alternatively, we can keep the following attitude while eating: 'I have offered this food to the Lord. He has eaten it and left His remnants for me to consume. It is now His prasad, which has been touched by His lips. Let me eat it while remembering His grace, and thereby enhance my devotion.'

It was along these lines that the great devotee, Uddhav, said to Shree Krishna:

tvayopabhukta-srag-gandha-vāso'laṅkāra-carcitāḥ
uchchhiṣhṭa-bhojino dāsās tava māyāṁ jayema hi
(Shreemad Bhagavatam 11.6.46)

'My Lord, I will eat the remnants of the food offered to You. I will offer all clothes and ornaments to You and wear them as Your prasad. I will use the leftovers of the perfumes that You were worshipped with. In this way, by Your mercy, I will overcome this maya, which is Yours and is so difficult to conquer.'

Consider another example. Sleeping is considered a very routine activity. But the karm yogi consecrates it at the altar of His Lord with the sentiment: 'My body is exhausted. I will sleep so that it gets refreshed, and then, tomorrow again I can engage in bhakti.'

Alternatively, the karm yogi thinks: 'I need to fulfil the physical requirement of the body to sleep. Oh Lord, please come in my dream, and enhance my devotion by giving me Your remembrance even in my sleep.'

In this way, every work becomes connected with the divine. Jagadguru Shree Kripalu-ji Maharaj explained that we should not even scratch ourselves for our pleasure. Rather, if we have to scratch, we should think: 'Shree Krishna is standing in front of me and laughing at what I am doing. All right, Oh Lord! Be amused and laugh while I scratch myself.'

Let us take another mundane activity such as cleaning or sweeping the house. One sentiment of doing it could be: 'Oh how boring this is! My husband creates such a mess. My child turns his room into a pigsty.' But if we work with this outlook, it will remain a worldly chore and will not purify our mind.

Instead, we can replace mundane thoughts with devotional sentiments: 'My soul-beloved Lord Krishna will be coming to my home. Let me clean it well to make this abode fit for His dwelling.' This sentiment will transform the same household work into service for the Divine.

That is exactly what Shabari, the tribal lady in the Ramayan, used to do. Daily, she would wake up, thinking: 'Today Shree Ram will surely come to my home. Where should I make Him sit? Is this place good? No, that place is better. Should I feed Him this? No, I will feed Him that.' Immersing herself in such sentiments was her devotion. Every day, she would clean all the pathways to her hut and decorate her humble abode. The consequence was that Lord Ram came to her hut while He was going through the forest. When He did, she became so absorbed in loving devotion that she lost all sensibility. She tasted the berries to check if they were sour and then fed the half-eaten ones to Lord Ram. But God, who cares only for the love of the devotee, accepted those half-eaten berries offered by Shabari with great relish and commented, 'I have never tasted anything as delicious as these!'

The practice of karm yog requires the fulfilment of one important condition, which is the constant remembrance of God. This is the one instruction that has been repeated and emphasised above all else in the Bhagavad Gita. Arjun's plea was, 'I wish to abdicate my professional duty. It is too disturbing and confusing.' The response by Shree Krishna was, 'No, Arjun! Do your duties in sublime awareness.'

sarveshu kāleshu mām anusmara yudhya cha
(Bhagavad Gita 8.7)

'Remember Me at all times and continue to work.' Jagadguru Shree Kripalu-ji Maharaj also emphasised constant remembrance in his teachings:

mana hari meṅ tana jagata meṅ, karm yog yehi jāna
(*Bhakti Śhatak* verse 84)

'If the body is engaged in the world and the mind is in God, that is karm yog.' Saint Kabir taught the same principle in simple language:

sumirana kī sudhi yauṅ karo, jyoṅ surabhi suta māhiñ
kahe kabīra charo charata bisarata kabahunka nāhiñ

'Remember God as a cow remembers its calf. It grazes grass in the field all day but keeps its mind on the calf.'

But how can we constantly remember God while performing all our daily activities? Simply follow the easy technique explained next.

Practice of the Presence of God

Throughout our waking state, we have constant awareness of ourselves: 'I am eating. I am walking. I am thinking. I am speaking, etc.' We must now add the perception of the presence of God to our consciousness: 'I am not alone. God is always with me. Shree Krishna is watching me. He is my witness and my protector.' In fact, God is everywhere and all-pervading, but we forget to realise His presence. Now we need to make space for Him in our awareness and practise realising His constant presence with us.

Most of us do acknowledge the presence of God when we visit a temple, church, mosque, gurudwara, synagogue, etc. However, we forget Him as soon as we walk out of there. This partial concept—that God is present only in a place of worship—affects our attitude. It makes us develop a double standard—be virtuous and devotional in the temple, but when outside it, do as you wish. Because we limit our experience of God to just the temple, we lower our standard of good behaviour. Instead, if we realise that the whole world is His temple, and He is watching us everywhere, we would never indulge in sin anywhere. At all times, we would keep a high standard of ethics and morality.

How can we implement this technique in our daily routine? Let us say you go to your office and sit on your chair in the morning. Before beginning work, stop for a moment. First, visualise God seated on a chair in one corner of the room. Think, 'Shree Krishna is watching me. All I am doing is for His pleasure and in His service.' Now begin your work.

Since you are not yet an accomplished karm yogi, it is natural that as you get engrossed in your work, you will forget God. Never mind. After an hour, stop work for a moment and again think, 'He is watching me. He is saying, "Aay ... you were supposed to keep your mind in Me. What have you started thinking?"' In this way, your consciousness that had slipped will again get uplifted. The stream of fruitless thoughts that had begun flowing in your mind will stop.

Keep practising in this manner after every hour. Once you have solidified the practice at intervals of one hour, increase the frequency to every half hour. When that is achieved, increase the frequency further to intervals of fifteen minutes. With constant practice, you will reach a stage where you will continuously feel the presence of God with you.

We can compare the above technique with the game of cricket. When a Test cricketer comes to the crease to bat, he surveys the field. The reason is that a fast bowler's ball takes less than half a second to cross the twenty-two yards of the pitch. So, after the bowler releases the ball, there is not enough time for the batsman to see where the fielders are standing before hitting the ball. That is why, prior to taking his stance, the batsman looks at the field that has been set for him by the opposing team captain.

Then, with the positions of the eleven players in his mind, the batsman faces the bowler. When the ball reaches him, he skilfully guides it between two fielders. The commentator screams, 'The batsman has found the gap in the field. The ball has been placed between mid-wicket and mid-on and is crossing the boundary for four runs!'

How did the batsman accomplish such a skilful task? By keeping the positions of the eleven fielders in his mind and then playing his shot. The practice of karm yog is far simpler than that. It does not require us to keep eleven personalities in our mind. Simply remember one, your Eternal Father, at all times, and do your work.

Purity of Intention Removes Stress

We had discussed that attachment to outcomes is the primary reason for stress. The practice of karm yog naturally eliminates stress by destroying its root cause. In it, we do everything for God's pleasure. After our best efforts, if we do not get the results we desire, we think, 'It was probably not the will of God. Let me submit to His wish and be happy.' This detachment from outcomes frees us from stress, anxiety, tension and fear.

Let me give a personal example to illustrate this point:

Before I began visiting the US, I used to deliver a 15–20 days' lecture series in India. I had a team of boys who were fully dedicated to the cause of service to God and guru. Living with me, they would practise their sadhana and help in the mission.

The leader of the team was a dynamic young man. He would go to the next town beforehand and finalise the programme. He would then get the publicity material prepared. The paṇḍāl *(tent for the programme) would be arranged for an audience of about five thousand people. Then the entire team would reach the new town a week ahead of the programme. They would create a publicity blitzkrieg by putting up scores of billboards and thousands of wall posters. They would also distribute tens of thousands of leaflets.*

Usually, the programme would succeed, and we would get the targeted number of people in the audience. But sometimes it would fail. When the programme torpedoed and the attendance was sparse, my team leader would feel shattered. He would start crying. For me, it was difficult to see an energetic youth cry. I would ask him, 'Why are you so upset?'

He would respond, 'Swami-ji, we tried so hard but people did not come.'

I would then explain to him, 'For whom did you try? Was it for yourself or the pleasure of God? If you were working so hard as a service to God, then there is no reason to be upset. You put in your best efforts, and after that, the results were in the hands of God. To be upset means you were attached to the results; in other words, you were working for your own pleasure, not God's. And if you were truly doing this as an offering to the Lord, then think that if the results are not as expected, then it must not be His will. Be content by thinking in this manner. Of course, we must always introspect to see if there was anything better we could have done. But then, learn your lessons and move ahead.'

Thus, stress disappears when we offer the fruits of our exertions to God because we see our work as a service to Him. Consequently, we exert ourselves to the best of our ability for the pleasure of God. Then work becomes joyful and not a grind to bear.

When our intention is purified, we see ourselves as servants of God. Based on this knowledge, we develop a healthy self-identity. Such a sense of identity does not arise from the ego; instead, it is based upon thinking of ourselves as the tiny soul that is the eternal servitor of God. In this manner, we maintain humility without being self-demeaning. Additionally, we realise that His grace makes all things possible, and we are freed from the 'pride of doership'.

The purity of purpose also improves our interpersonal interactions. Recognising the divinity in others helps us maintain a healthy attitude towards all. Most importantly, even while performing our worldly tasks, we move towards the goal of God-realisation.

Such purity of purpose attracts the abundant grace of God. To get an inkling of the abundance of God, behold the vastness of the enormous universe we live in. We simply need to stand under the starlit sky at night to realise how tiny we are and how immense His creation is. Zeroing in from the macrocosm, we come to the microcosm. Here, too, we find tremenduous variety in every drop of creation. There are millions of species of life, each with their unique characteristics and specialities. Within each species, there is so much of variety. We see how all humans, more than seven billion of us, have different looks, fingerprints, voices and attitudes. The same immensity in variety exists in other species as well. No two leaves of a tree are exactly alike.

The Bhagavad Gita says that all this is but a speck of God's splendour. This implies that the enormity of God's personality is simply mind-boggling. He is infinite in every way, and most importantly for us, His grace is also infinite. The only thing that comes in the way of our receiving it is our lack of purity. As we keep purifying our intent, we naturally attract more and more of His divine grace.

Conclusion

In this chapter, we discussed that to achieve success in life, we need purity of intention. Without it, we will be like a speeding vehicle without brakes. We learnt that impure intention is the cause of stress, anxiety, fear, etc. In contrast, pure intention is the panacea for all negative sentiments. We also discussed how purity of intention is inbuilt into the practice of karm yog. In it, we do everything for the pleasure of God. This enables us to internally keep the mind in perfect equilibrium, while externally engaging in all kinds of complex tasks.

Here, it is pertinent to draw attention to one vital aspect of the practice of karm yog. Success in karm yog is in direct proportion to the extent of love we develop for the Divine Lord. The more love we possess for Him, the easier it will become for us to keep the mind absorbed in Him.

What, then, is the way to develop love for God? Any technique requires knowledge of the methodology for its development and implementation. Surprising as it may seem, love for God also grows with divine knowledge. Accordingly, we now come to the fifth mindset for success, happiness and fulfilment, which is the mindset of 'cultivating knowledge'.

CHAPTER 5

THE MINDSET OF
CULTIVATING KNOWLEDGE

In the previous chapter, we saw how purity of intention lifts our mind above negative emotions. But mere intention is not enough. As the saying goes: 'The road to hell is paved with good intentions.' Many have the best intentions but fail to take the right action because they do not have the requisite knowledge. Many well-intended ventures are launched every year. Sadly, statistics reveal that four out of five start-ups fail. Those who failed also intended to succeed, but they did not possess the technique—the knowledge—for doing it correctly. This brings us to the mindset of acquiring the proper knowledge for accomplishing success, happiness and fulfilment.

Some people say that knowledge is not really necessary, and the power of intention is sufficient. They profess that if we sincerely desire something, we will surely attain it. They go by the statement: 'You are in life where you wish to be.' However, while this statement may seem nice to read, it is far from the truth. Let me share my experience on this topic with you.

Once, we were driving in the state of Odisha, India, from one town to another. We started from Phulbani and intended to go to Bhawanipatna. Along the way, near Boudh, we lost our bearings. So, we stopped and asked the owner of the nearby petrol station for directions. He was very kind and explained the way in detail and even made a map for us. We proceeded with the map, but after two-and-a-half hours we landed up in Sambalpur. What had gone wrong?

We had intended to be in Bhawanipatna and we had even put in our earnest effort. But mere intention was not enough. The problem was that the map made by the petrol pump owner was wrong. Lack of proper knowledge had caused our undoing. The maxim, 'You are in life where you intend to be,' was proved incorrect to us on that day.

Thus, purity of intention is insufficient for accomplishment; it needs the support of the mindset of knowledge. If you wish to play golf, a positive attitude will surely be helpful for better performance. However, if you do not know the technique of executing the shot, no amount of positive thinking will carry the ball over the pond, through the thistles and around the sand trap.

There are numerous bankruptcies filed every year by people who conceived 'brilliant' ideas for success. They had the purest of intentions and believed with all their heart that they could achieve their goals. But what they lacked was technique.

Some people claim: 'Ignorance is bliss.' But if ignorance is bliss, then why are the ignorant, the uneducated and the unintelligent miserable? Ignorance is not bliss; ignorance is misery, disease, pain and agony. Let me narrate a funny story to illustrate the point:

I heard of a married couple who was returning from the funeral of their Uncle Dharmendra. He had lived with them for twenty years. He had been such a nuisance that he had almost succeeded in ruining their marriage.

'There is something I have to say to you, dear,' said the husband. 'If it hadn't been for my love for you, I wouldn't have put up with your Uncle Dharmendra for a single day.'

'My Uncle Dharmendra!' the wife exclaimed in horror. 'I thought he was your uncle!' They both realised that due to ignorance they had suffered for twenty years.

For this couple, ignorance was definitely not bliss. They had made a false assumption without bothering to find out the truth, and it had brought twenty years of suffering upon them. What was the cause of suffering? Ignorance!

Here is another story highlighting the anguish of ignorance.

A patient went to a doctor as his stomach was griping terribly and he was in immense pain. On reaching the clinic, he found that the doctor was not in. So, he waited in his chamber, but the pain in his abdomen was unbearable.

Finally, after an hour, the doctor walked in. He checked the patient, prescribed medicine and asked the pharmacist to dispense it. The patient exclaimed, 'Oh doctor, the medicine was with the pharmacist all along. Due to my ignorance of what the right medicine was, I suffered indescribable misery for an hour while waiting for you to arrive.'

The doctor responded, 'Ignorance is the reason for all our suffering. If only we can get the proper knowledge, misery disappears.'

The doctor had echoed the profound words of Sage Ved Vyas:

ajñānamevāsya hi mūla kāraṇam (*Adhyātma Rāmāyaṇ*)

'The cause of suffering in all human beings is their lack of knowledge.' Thus, the journey of life is a movement from the darkness of ignorance to the light of wisdom.

Theoretical Knowledge Precedes Practical Implementation

Any technique needs knowledge for its understanding and implementation. Without it, we grope and flounder in the dark. In the absence of a better direction, we have to rely upon guesswork, experimentation and hearsay. Instead, if we have proper knowledge, it reveals to us the best and most effective way to do what we want.

Hence, theory precedes practical in all spheres of life. To do something well requires theoretical knowledge. The better the quality of our knowledge, the more effective we are at any task. This is true for both material and spiritual endeavours.

Nowadays, most people try to provide the best education to their children. Typically, the first quarter of one's life is spent in acquiring knowledge. That is because parents realise that the quality of their children's lives will depend upon the quality of the knowledge they acquire in school and college.

Similarly, developing countries pay huge amounts to purchase technology from developed countries. They need specialised know-how and realise that it comes at a price. They pay for the expertise because they know that quality knowledge can make the difference between success and failure. Even one nugget of wisdom can give them the edge, as the following story illustrates:

Alphatel, a company in an underdeveloped country, desired to set up a factory for manufacturing mobile phones. Its executives contacted Deutsche Telecom, a German corporation, for the purchase of technology. Deutsche Telecom offered to do a turnkey project. It is a project where the supplier sets up the entire plant, and the customer is only required to turn the key for starting it. The project came with a one-year guarantee on the functioning of the factory.

For one year, the factory functioned well. But the moment it entered the thirteenth month, the biggest machine in the production line came to a grinding halt.

Alphatel reached out to Deutsche Telecom for service support. They were told that a service engineer would come down from Germany, but it would be a billed visit since they were now out of warranty.

The engineer came over for a service visit. He looked around the plant, tapped some machines while putting his ear to them, and listened to the vibrations. Finally, he found a screw loose. He tightened it, and whirr ... The production line began rolling.

'That will be one hundred thousand Deutsche Marks,' said the service engineer.

'What? One hundred thousand for tightening one screw!' the executives of Alphatel were outraged.

'One hundred thousand is not for tightening the screw,' said the engineer. 'It is for knowing which screw needed to be tightened. For that piece of knowledge, I did post-graduation in engineering and then an additional specialisation in mobile technology. Plus, I gathered experience at Deutsche Telecom for the last fifteen years.'

The above story illustrates the difference that even one bit of information can make. Very often, a small improvement in the way we think or the way we do a particular task can lead to a considerable enhancement in our performance. Sometimes, a single idea changes people's careers or an entire industry. One useful tip in sports helps players rise to the top. One crucial bit of information related to health transforms a sick person's life. Hence, those who develop the mindset of seeking out new and useful knowledge in their fields are the ones who get ahead.

The power of knowledge can be utilised by everyone for their benefit. But sadly, this simple truth is ignored by millions. Statistics reveal that 33 per cent of Americans do not ever read a book from cover to cover again, after passing out of college. They mistakenly assume that since they possess a degree from a university, they now have all the knowledge they need for a successful life.

In contrast, those with the mindset of knowledge keep learning at every opportunity. Using their grasping power, they gather information from various sources and quickly develop the skillsets required for excellence in their field of work.

In today's world, accessibility to information has become so widespread that it is not even necessary to go through years of education to get the knowledge one requires. Information is available on a variety of online platforms and simply needs to be accessed. Those who realise the importance of knowledge keep upgrading theirs and rapidly rise to higher levels of excellence.

Information Explosion in Modern Times

In the last two thousand years of modern history, the last few decades have seen extraordinary growth in the combined knowledge of humankind. Seven hundred years ago, Roger Bacon, an English philosopher, was considered by his society as a person who knew everything worth knowing. He was believed to be up-to-date with all the knowledge and science available at that time. However, in today's world of information technology, it is impossible for anybody to be well-versed, with complete knowledge, even in one subject.

This explosion of knowledge is the result of multiple forces collating together. Firstly, the World Wide Web has unleashed the information revolution. The internet provides us access to millions of websites around the world, containing the accumulated information of more than half-a-million libraries. Further, the development of mobile technology has put access to that information at our fingertips.

Secondly, technological advances have led to the development of high-speed computers for processing the available information. Every other person nowadays owns a laptop or a desktop computer with the ability to multitask at amazing speeds and with much ease.

Thirdly, the growth in communication has enabled knowledge to be shared at breakneck speeds. A single 'send' command on your email browser can transmit the message straight from your office to the email boxes of thousands of people around the world. Social media has enhanced this even further. You can reach tens of millions of people within the few seconds you take to create and post a message on your Facebook, Twitter or Instagram account.

The consequence is that the knowledge generated by researchers in one field is instantaneously available to scientists in other fields. Further, they have the technology to save it, process it, work on it and utilise it in their respective areas of specialisation. This is resulting in a synergy that is doubling and tripling the knowledge of humankind at breathtaking speeds.

These three forces—information, technology and communication—working together are opening up ever-new possibilities for people to utilise the available knowledge for achieving their goals. And this is only the beginning because the rate of change is accelerating every year—in fact, every day. It is like a glacier that has begun moving and will keep moving at an exponential rate. The option to stop it does not exist. The decision we need to make is whether we adapt to this change or become victims of it.

If we wish to ride the tide of change, we must not be possessors of outdated expertise. We must develop a thirst to constantly upgrade our skills by utilising material that is so readily available on various online platforms.

However, the distinction between information and knowledge needs to be borne in mind. Information per se will not benefit us. We will benefit from our ability to generate useful knowledge from that information. People who have this skill are riding the new economy of the world, which we shall discuss next.

The Knowledge Economy

Sociologists have given names to the different ages through which human society has evolved over the last three hundred years. Until around AD 1750, the Agricultural Age had prevailed in most parts of the world. Society was structured as an agricultural economy, where 90 per cent of the people lived in villages and were engaged in professions related to farming.

Then came the Industrial Age, which saw the establishment of factories for the production of commodities. It led to a rapid increase of population in cities. These developments transitioned society into a manufacturing economy. Now, dominion over the world lay in the hands of those who had better manufacturing processes. Ralph Waldo Emerson expressed the spirit of the Industrial Age in his famous quote: 'Build a better mousetrap; the world will beat a path to your door.'

But over time, access to the processes of manufacturing became commonplace. The products manufactured were almost identical in quality amongst most producers. Thus, the relative importance of manufacturing in society reduced. The world then entered the Marketing Age. Distinction was achieved by marketing, and those with better promotional ideas moved up the economic ladder.

With the development of the personal computer in the 1980s, society changed rapidly again. Computers empowered people across various strata of society to process data and store it for the future. Distinction in society now hinged upon the quality of information that people had access to. This engendered humankind into the Information Age.

But now the pace of transformation accelerated even further. By the turn of the millennium, availability of information had also become commonplace. It no longer remained the differentiating factor between the haves and have-nots. The importance shifted to producing useful knowledge from the readily available information. Consequently, we are seeing the world economic structure gradually transition to the Knowledge Age. This age is characterised by the use of knowledge to create tangible and intangible value. Thus, knowledge has become the most important capital resource, more than even finances and machinery.

Throughout history, economic value was contained in finances, land, human labour, machinery, fixtures and other hard assets. Nations fought wars to gain control over assets. The individuals who powered the economy were the ones who combined all these hard assets to create products and services for the marketplace. All that has changed in the present times. Now, the biggest source of value is knowledge, information and ideas.

In this new scenario, your greatest wealth could be in your own head—brilliant ideas and concepts. Many of the biggest enterprises dominating the world today were instituted by people who started with nothing. They simply came up with a grand idea that revolutionised their industry. Hence, the best opportunities today lie in deep contemplative and reflective work powered by your knowledge and thoughts. In this changed scenario, even if your office building burns down, you could walk away and build your business once again with your intellectual property.

Sociologists have coined the phrase 'Knowledge Economy' to describe the latest stage in economic restructuring. Information is readily available to the masses. But, people need more than that to succeed. They need to locate information quickly, and then process it to think, learn, innovate, and thereby create new knowledge. The most significant assets now are your ability to think and apply that thought process to get results that others will value.

In the old economy, people toiled for years to accumulate the capital for starting a successful manufacturing business or service enterprise. In the new economy, with the biggest capital being inside your head, it does not take long for someone smart enough to succeed. The importance of intellectual capital has risen so rapidly that banks are still grappling with how to put a value on it. Earlier, for extending loans, they estimated the collateral from the hard assets of the borrower. In the present scenario, the borrowers' assets may be intangible. They may lie in the borrowers' ability to think and create or add value.

In the old economy, there were a limited amount of physical assets that were divided among different stakeholders. Scarcity of resources has been the cause of so many wars in human history. In contrast, the characteristics of a knowledge economy are not of scarcity, but abundance. The wonderful thing about knowledge is that it can be reproduced thousands of times, without it diminishing. On the contrary, the more knowledge is shared, the further it grows. As it reaches a variety of experts and specialists, it develops more facets.

The growth of communication has further added to this scenario. Any new idea that you develop can be disseminated around the world in no time, with the click of a mouse. Thus, the limitation of the geographic location has also been diminished. You could be on a cruise ship, or a mountain cabin or even in a plane, but if you have access to the internet, you could still be productively engaged in your business.

Thus, in the developing Knowledge Economy, the mindset of knowledge has become extremely important. One needs to learn how to gather information quickly, and then, through deep thought, transform it into useful knowledge.

While discussing the mindset of cultivating knowledge, we do need to bear in mind that material knowledge is not the only kind of knowledge that exists. **There is also spiritual knowledge, which is even more valuable and beneficial for success, happiness and fulfilment in life.**

At this point, people often ask the question: In the Knowledge Age, is spirituality still required, or has it become redundant? Now that we know so much, is there still any need to believe in God? And is not spiritual belief a sign of ignorance? These are common questions that arise in the minds of many. Let us address them.

The Need for Spiritual Knowledge

Amongst all the branches of knowledge developed on this planet, science occupies the pride of place. It is particularly appealing to the intellectual elite because it is based on logical arguments, quantifiable facts and verifiable procedures. Science is appealing to the masses as well because it raises our standard of living and provides us with luxury and comfort, which are important to all.

In the modern world, we practically worship science. On any topic or issue, the scientific opinion is considered indisputable and the last word on the matter. In this era of science, where does spirituality stand? Does it not contradict the scientific viewpoint? Do we have to choose between being scientific and spiritual? Is there any way we can converge these two branches of knowledge?

The reason why we talk of a convergence between science and spirituality is that a few hundred years ago, from the time of Copernicus and Galileo, a divergence arose between the two perspectives in the Western world. Each of these—science and spirituality—wanted to explain the entire field of knowledge from their viewpoint. This led to tremendous acrimony on both sides. And the result of this antagonism between science and spirituality is that today there is practically no overlap. You do not find a scientific paper stating that such-and-such phenomenon occurs because of the will of God.

This neglect of spirituality by science has led to an unpalatable situation today, where we find that although science has placed tremendous power in our hands—such as nuclear power and genetic bioengineering—it has not presented any ethical or moral system that can guide us regarding the proper use of that power. Science has enhanced our standard of living, but the resultant industrialisation has led to the rapid depletion of non-renewable energy and mineral resources. It has also caused a colossal deterioration of the ecosystem and the concomitant pollution of land, water and air.

One of the primary objectives of the pursuit of science was to remove the miseries of humankind and help us experience happiness and joy. However, for most of us, this has not happened. We would probably find that our great-grandfathers were happier than us, even though they possessed fewer material luxuries. Why is this so?

We all realise that happiness is not a function of the number of luxury goods we possess; it hinges upon the peace and harmony within our mind. The Western philosopher, John Milton, put it so well when he said:

The mind is its own place, and in itself
Can make a Heaven of Hell, a Hell of Heaven.

(*Paradise Lost*)

If that is the case, then what is the method of controlling and managing our mind? This technology does not exist in science. That is why the greatest scientist of the last century, Albert Einstein, had said:

Science has succeeded in denaturing the plutonium atom.
But it cannot denature the evil in man's heart.

This is where spiritual science comes in. It is that body of knowledge which gives us the tools to purify our mind and intellect, and thereby lead a noble and divine life. Through it, we learn to control our thoughts and make them lofty and sublime. It also teaches us ethics and morality without which we humans would fall to the level of animals. As a result, spiritual knowledge too has its relevance and importance in human life.

Spiritual knowledge is also necessary for another crucial purpose. Let us discuss it next.

The Search for the Absolute Truth

People undertook the pursuit of science, not merely for its practical utility, but also to know the Absolute Truth. We looked upon science as a means for solving the mystery of life and creation. We wished to know who we are. Why are we on this planet? Why does creation exist? And what is the purpose of our life? However, even with all the advancement of scientific theory, these questions remain unanswered.

One of the reasons for it is that science is still a work-in-progress. Consequently, its concepts keep changing. In the evolution of science, theories were propounded by great scientists and were accepted as the Truth by their contemporaries. But then other scientists came along who discredited the old theories or proved them to be inadequate and established newer ones. This leads us to believe that with further advancement in science, theories accepted as the Truth today may be disbanded tomorrow. Hence, if our goal is to know the Absolute Truth in the short lifespan we have, then science as a methodology is insufficient.

To elucidate this point, let me take you on a brief journey through the evolution of science over the last three hundred and fifty years or so. Around the year 1675, Sir Isaac Newton presented his Laws of Motion. At that time, they were accepted as the ultimate Truth on the subject. Newton stated that space is three-dimensional; time flows through space without mingling with it in any way; force is proportional to mass and distance and it acts instantaneously between two points. So, from the perspective of Newtonian mechanics, the entire world was like a huge machine. If we knew the present moment and found out all the forces at work, the next moment could be perfectly predicted.

However, after Newton came Michael Faraday. He passed a magnet through a wire and produced electric current. By doing so, he went beyond Newton's Laws of Motion and presented a higher level of understanding of the physical phenomena in the universe.

Faraday was succeeded by J.C. Maxwell. He replaced the concept of force with that of the force field. He stated that a proton with a positive charge has a force field around it, irrespective of any negative charge nearby. This led to a new comprehension about the nature of light energy. Light now came to be understood as a rapidly oscillating electromagnetic spectrum.

After Maxwell came the famous Albert Einstein, with his Theory of Relativity. He postulated that space and time are not independent but relative to each other. Two observers moving at different velocities will sequence events differently on their timeline. He also stated that matter at rest possesses energy; the amount of that energy is described by his famous equation $E = mc^2$.

At the same time, there were advances taking place in the field of chemistry. You may remember reading in school about Ernest Rutherford's periodic table. Rutherford bombarded atoms with alpha particles and measured the counts with a Geiger counter. He found that the atom is not a solid particle as it was previously understood to be, instead, it consists of tremendous amounts of empty space. In fact, 99.99 per cent of an atom is vacant space.

His proposition was altered by the quantum physicists. Around the 1920s, Niels Bohr and his fellow scientists came up with the Quantum Theory. They stated that, at the subatomic level, matter is not what we think it is, and the classical concept of it being a solid mass is wrong. Subatomic matter does not exist at places but only shows tendencies to exist. Now the whole idea of matter changed to an energy field. When Einstein heard of this, he was unable to come to terms with the new findings. In his famous book, *Tao of Physics*, Fritjof Capra quotes Einstein as confessing:

My every attempt to adapt the theoretical concepts of physics to the new kind of knowledge failed. It was as if the ground had been pulled from one's feet with nothing to fall upon.

Along the same lines, Werner Heisenberg, one of the quantum physicists himself, stated:

The violent reactions to the new developments of modern science can only be understood when one realises that here the foundations have started moving, and that this motion has caused the feeling that the ground would be cut from science.

The second problem that arose was of synthesising the Quantum Theory with Einstein's relativity models because at the subatomic level, particles move at tremendous speed. The electron orbits at 2,200 kilometres per second while the proton has an extremely rapid spin or intrinsic angular momentum. So, there was now a need to reconcile Einstein's theory with the Quantum Theory. However, such a theory has not yet been developed. And if we do come up with one, there is no guarantee another theory will not supersede it after a few decades.

Since the days of Einstein and the quantum physicists, scientists have been in search of a Unified Field Theory that would tie all forces, masses and energies in one equation. But so far, they are nowhere close to finding it. Astonishingly, a unified field theory was mentioned five thousand years ago in the Bhagavad Gita:

bhūmirāpo 'nalo vāyuḥ khaṁ mano buddhir eva cha
ahankāra itīyaṁ me bhinnā prakṛitir aṣhṭadhā (7.4)

Lord Krishna said to Arjun: 'Earth, water, fire, air, space, mind, intellect and ego—these are all different aspects of God's material energy.' In other words, Einstein had merely discovered that matter is a form of energy. The Bhagavad Gita elucidates, way beyond Einstein's theory, that all entities in creation—earth, water, fire, air, space, etc.—are different forms of God's energy.

We see how spiritual science possesses deep insight into the nature of force, matter and energy—topics that have puzzled scientists for over a century. It only goes to show that science would do well to take spiritual knowledge more seriously.

Limitations of Scientific Knowledge

The reason why scientists do not give credence to spiritual knowledge is that they feel it relies upon faith. But they do not realise that scientific knowledge is also developed based on beliefs and assumptions.

For instance, Newtonian mechanics was founded on the assumptions of Euclidean geometry. Remember the geometry you learnt in school? It had certain postulates. For example, the first postulate of Euclid states: 'Given two points in space, there is only one line that can pass through both of them.' This was a hypothesis that Euclid, an ancient Greek mathematician, had made, without any concrete proof, and Newton incorporated it in his theories.

Later, a German mathematician named Bernhard Riemann changed Euclid's first postulate, and stated: 'Given two points in space, there are two or more lines that can pass through them.' He then proceeded to develop an entire Riemannian geometry.

Another Russian mathematician, Nikolai Lobachevsky, relooked at Euclid's fifth postulate, which states: 'Given a line and a point, there is only one line that can be drawn through that point parallel to the first line.' In its place, Lobachevsky postulated: 'Given a line and a point, there are two or more lines that can be drawn through that point parallel to the first line.' With this assumption, Lobachevsky's geometry was developed. Einstein, in his Theory of Relativity, utilised Lobachevsky's postulates.

Thus, we see that even in science, we start with postulates that are merely assumed to be true. The assumptions are unproven and could as well be false. Professor Charles H. Townes, Nobel Prize winner for physics (1964), expressed this very well:

Science itself requires faith. We don't know if our logic is correct. I don't know you are there. You don't know I am here. We may just be imagining all this, you see. I have faith that the world is what it seems like, and thus, I believe you are there. I can't prove it from any fundamental point of view ... Yet, I have to accept a certain framework in which to operate. The idea that 'religion is faith' and 'science is knowledge', I think, is quite wrong. We scientists believe in the existence of the external world and the validity of our own logic. We feel quite comfortable about it. Nevertheless, these are acts of faith. We can't prove them.

In his book *Man the Unknown*, Alexis Carrel, a French surgeon and biologist who won the Nobel Prize for physiology in 1912, states:

> Our mind has a natural tendency to reject the things that do not fit into the frame of scientific or philosophical beliefs of our time. After all, scientists are only men. They are saturated with the prejudices of their environment and epoch. They willingly believe that facts that cannot be explained by current theories do not exist. At present times, scientists still look upon telepathy and other metaphysical phenomena as illusions. Evident facts having an unorthodox appearance are suppressed.

Here I do not wish to denigrate science, but merely show its limitations in the quest for the Absolute Truth, thereby establishing the need for another kind of knowledge, which is spiritual knowledge.

Knowledge of the Self

Now, we come to the most basic question, 'Who are we?' Does science know the answer to this? It has conveniently assumed that the body is a combination of atoms and molecules, and nothing more. Hence, it understands the 'self' to be the sum total of the chemicals that compose the body. It thus assumes that when the body is destroyed, the 'self' will also cease to exist.

Scientists, in general, have blindly believed the above premise. However, I would like to question the presumption, 'Mr Scientist, if we are merely a bunch of atoms and molecules, then where does free will come from?' No answer will be forthcoming to explain the freedom of choice that we possess.

A famous Austrian scientist, Erwin Schrodinger, Nobel Prize winner in physics (1933), and the propagator of the famous Schrodinger equation, had observed this fallacy and stated:

The cells of my body work in accordance with the laws of nature. And yet I know that I control these cells, forcing the effects and taking responsibility for the actions. It seems these two statements can only be reconciled if there is an 'I' separate from these atoms and molecules, which is guiding their motion in accordance with laws of nature.

Similarly, Thomas Huxley, an English biologist, said:

If you were to ask a scientist whether they believe in religion or spirituality, invariably they would say they do not believe. And if you were to ask them, 'Do you possess a free will?' they would say, 'Yes, we do.' Intuitively we all know we do possess a free will. Yet, in the laws of nature known today, there is no scope for free will. Yet, all scientists do realise that we do possess the freedom to choose. This or that.

Today, there are legions of consciousness philosophers who, realising this lacuna in scientific thought, try to come up with alternative explanations for the source of consciousness in the body. Albert Szent-Györgyi, a Hungarian biochemist and Nobel Prize winner in physiology (1937), said:

In my search for the basis of consciousness, I ended up with atoms and molecules. Somewhere along the line, life slipped out of my hands. Now, in my old age, I am tracing my steps backward.

The unproven postulate of science is that the self is merely a bunch of chemicals. Spiritual science starts with a different postulate regarding the nature of the 'self'. The Vedas inform us that within this body is the spiritual soul, which gives us the identity we call 'I'. Life, or consciousness, is the symptom of the soul. As long as the soul is present in the body, it possesses sentience. Once the soul leaves, the body again transforms into insentient matter—the hands, feet, cells and molecules—because life is no longer present.

The Bhagavad Gita states:

kṣhetra-kṣhetrajñayor jñānaṁ (13.3)

'To understand the difference between the body, which is the field of activities, and the soul, which is the knower of the field, is true knowledge.' Thus, we are not merely a bag of chemicals; we are spiritual beings, free and eternally blessed souls.

Just as knowledge about the self is provided by spirituality, knowledge about God is also provided by it.

How the World Came into Existence

Now, let us take a look at another postulate blindly assumed by science. All scientific theory has been developed on the hypothesis that there is no God. However, this is an unverifiable premise. It can only be proven if we know all there is to know about everything that exists in the universe. If we do not know even one thing, it is possible that the one thing is God. Hence, until we know everything, we cannot prove that there is no God.

Yet, science has conveniently assumed that there is no God. Accordingly, it teaches that the world came into existence by accident. The prevailing theory is called the 'Big Bang Theory'. It claims that the universe existed as a mass of matter that was at a very high-density and high-temperature state. This mass exploded by itself, scattered and cooled down, and the world came into existence.

What the Big Bang Theory does not explain is how the laws of physics and chemistry came about. A bang should have created chaos and disorder. Why, then, do we see such intricate order prevailing in the universe? This goes against our innate logic. Is it not more reasonable to assume that there is a Supreme Intelligent Being behind this wonderful creation? The following story illustrates this:

There was once, in a high school, a geography teacher. He taught his students that the world was created automatically by an uncontrolled explosion that resulted in matter flying out and then cooling down. And thus, all of us humans are nothing more than stardust. At the end of the class, he gave an assignment to his students as homework. 'Please draw a map of the earth and bring it with you tomorrow.'

The students tried in their own way. Some copied the map from different atlases and others sketched it freehand. One student was of a philosophic bent of mind and unwilling to take the teacher's words at face value. He took a scrap of paper, scribbled some lines on it, and threw in some colours. The next day, when the students were submitting their maps, he too slipped his assignment into the pile on the teacher's desk.

The teacher came to the class. He began checking the assignments and marking them, until he came to that scrap of paper. On seeing it, he became infuriated. 'Who made this?' he yelled. The whole class was silent. He repeated the question, 'Tell me, whose handiwork is this?' Still everybody was quiet. He said, 'If nobody owns up for this, I will punish the entire class.'

Now the boy who had created it stood up. He said, 'Sir, in my opinion, nobody has made it.'

'What do you mean?' asked the exasperated teacher.

'I think the paper flew in and landed on your desk. The pencil flew in and lines were drawn. The colours flew in and dropped on the piece of paper. That is how this was created.'

The teacher said, 'What rubbish are you talking? How can this be made by itself? Definitely somebody has made it, and I suspect it is you who has done it.'

The boy replied, 'Sir, you are not willing to believe that a grotesque apparition of the map of the planet earth could be made by itself. And you want us to believe that the real thing consisting of innumerable planetary systems and galaxies has been created by itself! If this map requires a maker, then doesn't the real thing require an even more powerful and intelligent creator?'

Many famous scientists wholeheartedly agree with the above logic establishing the existence of God. Unfortunately, their views are not reflected in the body of science. Prof. Werner Arber, a Swiss microbiologist and geneticist who received the Nobel Prize in physiology in 1978 said:

Even the most primitive of cells requires the combination of several hundred macromolecules. How all these came together remains a mystery to me. The existence of a Creator, or God, seems a logical explanation for this.

Sir Isaac Newton himself said:

This most beautiful system of the sun, planets and comets could only proceed from the council and dominion of an intelligent and powerful being.

Albert Einstein also concluded:

Try and penetrate with our limited means the secrets of nature and you will find that, behind all the discernible concatenations, there remains something subtle, intangible and inexplicable. Veneration for this force behind anything that we can comprehend is my religion. To that extent I am, in point of fact, religious.

We see that science has made an unproven assumption that there is no superior intelligence responsible for creation. However, some of the greatest scientists have agreed that creation came about through the council and dominion of an all-intelligent Being, thereby endorsing the assumption of spirituality. If we respect science, then we should be willing to accept spirituality as a perfectly valid system of knowledge and thought as well.

The Synthesis of Science and Spirituality

In the Western world, the antagonism between science and religion stretches back to a few centuries. It was ignited by Nicolaus Copernicus in the early 16th century when he propounded the heliocentric theory of the universe. It proclaimed that all celestial bodies revolve around the sun, and not the earth as formerly believed. Around 1514, Copernicus completed a written work, *Commentariolus* (Latin for 'little commentary'), a forty-page manuscript that summarised his heliocentric theory and alluded to forthcoming mathematical formulas meant to serve as proof. He then published a second book, *De Revolutionibus Orbium Coelestium* ('on the revolutions of the celestial spheres') in which he detailed his theory as an alternative to Ptolemy's geocentric theory that had been widely accepted since ancient times.

Copernicus died soon after publishing his second book. However, his theories incensed the Vatican and were considered heretical. The leader of the Reformation movement, Martin Luther, also voiced his opposition to the heliocentric solar system model. Nevertheless, Copernicus' heliocentric theory had already caused waves in society. In AD 1600, an Italian priest, Giordano Bruno, who was also a philosopher, poet, mathematician and cosmological theorist, was sentenced to death. He was burnt at the stake because he refused to toe the purely religious line, and instead believed in freely mixing science and religion.

It was about a century after Copernicus that Galileo invented the Galilean telescope. He confirmed the conclusions of Copernicus through his astronomical observations. In 1616, Galileo went to Rome to try and persuade the Roman Catholic Church not to ban Copernicus' works. However, his efforts met with failure, and Galileo was found 'vehemently suspect of heresy'. A decree titled 'Holy Congregation for the Index' was issued to inform the public that the idea of the sun standing still and the earth moving around it was wholly false. Galileo was asked to 'abjure, curse, and detest' his opinion.

Galileo did retract his statements as he was ordained, but the scientific community had already latched on to his ideas. For the next two centuries, people were torn between the two divides—religion versus science. Later, evidence of Galileo's theories came through the accurate measurement of the stellar aberration of light by British astronomer James Bradley and the orbital motion of binary stars by William Herschel.

With the presentation of empirical proof by scientists, the debate regarding the astronomical configuration of the universe subsided. Subsequently, the Church adjusted its perspective to become more inclusive of modern scientific theories. However, in the minds of the general masses, the notion of antagonism between science and religion had been wedged, and it continues till today. Thus, a religious person is looked upon as irrational and illogical by the scientific community. Similarly, religious leaders remain suspicious and apprehensive of scientists.

From the Oriental perspective, there is no contradiction between science and spirituality. The *Muṇḍakopaniṣhad* states:

dve vidye veditavye parā chaivāparā cha   (1.1.4)

'There are two branches of knowledge—material science and spiritual science.' Both are valid and bona fide. In fact, the synthesis of both is necessary for making our life a success. Material knowledge—what we call modern science—enables us to understand external nature and harness it for the sustenance of our body. Spiritual knowledge helps us comprehend our inner self—the mind, intellect and ego—and purify it to manifest the divinity of the soul within. Thus, both science and spirituality are valid and bona fide areas of knowledge, and both are relevant to our lives. Just as a train travels on two rails, if we wish to make our life successful, we will have to utilise both these sciences.

Unfortunately, some spiritualists and materialists often have a singular perspective on this topic. Spiritualists look upon material science as evil that should be shunned, while materialists look upon spirituality as unnecessary superstition that should be done away with. The fact is that both these polarised views are fallacious.

Spiritualists who say, 'Material knowledge is useless', are mistaken. Without material science, how will we provide our body with its needs for nutrition, medicine and hygiene? A beautiful story illustrates this:

This incident is from the life of Gautam Buddha, before his enlightenment. He was sitting in meditation, having given up eating and sleeping. Many days went by, and he began feeling weak due to continuous fasting.

Some village women were passing by, singing a song. The words of the song fell on the Buddha's ears. They were singing, 'Tighten the strings of the tanpura but do not tighten them so much that the strings break.' The tanpura is a stringed musical instrument akin to the guitar.

When the Buddha heard the song, he thought, 'These illiterate village women are speaking such words of wisdom. If the strings are not tightened, the tanpura does not create the desired melodious sounds. But if they are overstretched, they snap.'

Similarly, we too must tighten the body, but not so much that it gets destroyed. We must practise austerity, but not to the extent that it permanently damages the body. Ayurveda states:

śharīra mādhyaṁ khalu dharma sādhanam
                                    (*Charak Samhita*)

'Our body is a medium for practising spirituality.' Thus, even to go towards God, we need the body, and that requires material science. If spiritualists marginalise it, they are mistaken.

At the same time, spiritual knowledge is indispensable too, and if materialists claim that it is a waste of time, they are also mistaken. Without spiritual science, we cannot figure out the technology for the purification of the mind. Max Planck, a great German scientist, who won the Nobel Prize in physics in 1918, also recognised this need for spirituality. In his article *Where is Science Going?* he stated:

I think that the religious element of man's nature must be recognised and cultivated if all the powers of the human soul are to act together in perfect balance and harmony. It was not by accident that the greatest thinkers of all ages were also deeply religious souls, even though they made no public show of their religious feelings.

By itself, material science is devoid of values. It places enormous power in our hands but does not inform us how to discriminate between the good and bad use of that power. This is why there is such a hue and cry in modern society about the latest scientific research in the fields of nuclear power, warfare technologies, artificial intelligence, genetic engineering and stem cell creations. On issues of morality and ethics, the wisdom to deal with them comes from spirituality.

We have understood that any discussion on the mindset of knowledge can never be complete without touching upon the topic of spirituality. Having discussed material knowledge at the outset of this chapter, let us now turn our attention to spiritual science.

Importance of Knowledge on the Spiritual Path

The Vedic scriptures have a very beautiful perspective of spirituality. They view it not as blind faith but as the science of self-purification. Hence, like any other science, it requires knowledge for its practice. The Bhagavad Gita states:

nahi jñānena sadṛiśhaṁ pavitramiha vidyate   (4.38)

Lord Krishna said: 'O Arjun, there is nothing so pure in this world as divine knowledge.' He also said:

sarvaṁ jñāna-plavenaiva vṛijinaṁ santariṣhyasi   (4.36)

'Seat yourself in the boat of knowledge, and cross over the ocean of life and death.' Thus, knowledge has a compelling role to play in the practice of spirituality. It enlightens us about the nature of the self, the purpose of life and the technique for sadhana. It helps us understand our relationship with God and the process to establish it.

The impediment to spiritual realisation is the ignorance that has veiled us, as the following story reveals:

Chetan was the area sales manager for a multinational consumer company. He had gone to visit the retail outlets in his sales territory. It was night-time by the time he covered all of them. So, he stopped at a cheap restaurant for dinner. The restaurant manager guided Chetan to an empty table.

On the next table, an old man was seated with a youngster. Both were lost in their own thoughts, neither talking nor looking at each other. They were drinking away as if there would be no tomorrow. Chetan cast a glance at them and then got busy with the dinner that was served to him.

A few minutes went by, and suddenly, the old man asked the youngster on his table, 'Sonny, where do you live?'

'I.P. Extension, Delhi,' responded the youngster.

'Really! I live in I.P. Extension as well. What a coincidence!' said the old man. 'Where in I.P. Extension?'

Now, the young man seemed to be getting interested. 'Sir, I live in Navaniti Apartments.'

'You must be kidding,' said the senior. 'I live in Navaniti Apartments too. Which floor is your home?'

'Fourth floor,' said the youth.

'O my God!' exclaimed the elderly man. 'I live on the fourth floor as well. What is your house number?'

'Uncle, my house number is 421.'

'I cannot believe this,' said the man. 'I live in house no. 421 as well!'

On hearing this conversation, Chetan grew more and more astounded. How could these two have the same address and yet not know each other? He stared at their faces, puzzled.

Seeing the bewilderment of Chetan, the restaurant manager said to him, 'Sir, do not be astonished at their dialogue. They have done the same drama every week for the last two years. They are father and son but when they get drunk, they forget each other. That is why they were asking who the other person was.'

The same is the situation with our soul. The Vedas say, *amṛitasya vai putrāḥ.* 'God is our eternal Father, and we are His children.' But we have forgotten our loving relationship with Him and are suffering in the material ocean since endless lifetimes. The way to connect with God is by dispelling this ignorance with the light of knowledge.

Amazingly, divine knowledge is also a means of cultivating devotion. Consider the following example:

A man was walking on the street when he found a bejewelled ring. He picked it up hesitatingly, and thought, 'This is probably artificial jewellery. It must be worth fifty rupees.' Nevertheless, he put the ring in his pocket and returned home.

Next day, he took the ring to a goldsmith, and said, 'Sir, can you please value this ring for me?' The goldsmith checked it out with his touchstone, and said, 'This is 24-carat gold. It must be worth fifty thousand rupees.' On hearing this, the man's appreciation for the ring increased.

A few days went by and his uncle, who was a jeweller, came to stay with him. The man showed him the ring and enquired, 'Uncle, what do you estimate as the worth of this ring and the stone in it?' The uncle took the ring in his hands and exclaimed, 'My child, where did you get this? It is worth at least fifty lakh rupees.'

The man said, 'Uncle, do not joke with me.'

'I am not joking. Sell it to me; I will pay you forty lakh rupees right now.' This convinced the man that the ring was worth half a crore. He immediately fell in love with it. Now when he sees it, he gets immense satisfaction.

The ring was the same, the man was the same, and his vision was also the same. But when his knowledge was that the ring was worth fifty rupees, his love for it was negligible. When his understanding changed that it was worth fifty thousand rupees, his love correspondingly increased. And when he realised that it was worth half a crore, his love for it knew no bounds.

The example illustrates how love for an object grows with knowledge. In the same way, if we gain knowledge of God, we will naturally develop love for Him as well. Sage Tulsidas states:

jāneṅ binu na hoi paratītī, binu paratītī hoi nahiṅ prītī

(Ramayan)

'Without knowing God, we will not develop faith in Him; and without faith, we will not be able to love Him.' The more we comprehend who God is, what His relationship is with us, and what He wishes to give us, the more our love for Him will develop.

Thus, we have seen the various benefits of knowledge for spiritual attainment. The *Bhakti Rasāmṛit Sindhu* describes three levels of spiritual *sādhaks* (aspirants): superlative, mediocre and inferior.

śhāstre yuktau cha nipuṇaḥ sarvathā dṛiḍha-niśhchayaḥ
prauḍha-śhraddho 'dhikārī yaḥ sa bhaktāvuttamo mataḥ

(1.2.17)

'Superlative sādhaks are those who have both—deep faith in God plus knowledge of the scriptures.' On their spiritual journey, such seekers move ahead with great speed and surety. Negative influences, bad association, doubt, languor, etc. do not affect them.

yaḥ śhāstrādiṣhvanipuṇaḥ śhraddhāvān sa tu madhyamaḥ

(1.2.18)

'Mediocre sādhaks are those who have deep faith in God, but they do not possess the knowledge of the scriptures.' Such seekers are always vulnerable to the negative associations of the world. For example, if they are engaged in the devotion of Lord Krishna, and someone says something to create doubt in the divinity of their *iṣhṭa dev* (chosen form of God), their devotion will begin to wobble. Instead, if they had possessed scriptural knowledge, they would have brushed away any comments or suggestions inimical to their devotion.

yo bhavet komala śhraddhaḥ sa kaniṣhṭho nigadyate

(1.2.19)

'Inferior sādhaks are those who possess neither deep faith in God nor the theoretical knowledge of the scriptures.' They take two steps forward, but then are besieged by doubt and retract three steps. In this way, due to lack of knowledge and weak faith, they keep moving forward and backward.

Hence, the mindset of knowledge is essential for achieving success on the spiritual journey. Now, while getting material knowledge is not difficult—it is available to us through several avenues—the mysterious one is spiritual knowledge. What is the way to acquire or receive it?

The Way to Spiritual Knowledge

Having discussed different aspects of knowledge, we will now discuss the one remaining question: How can we acquire divine knowledge? The first reference point for it are the Vedas.

bhūtaṁ bhavyaṁ bhaviṣhyaṁ cha sarvaṁ vedāt prasidhyati
(*Manu Smṛiti* 12.97)

'The veracity of any spiritual principle related to the past, present or the future is established on the basis of the Vedas.' These Vedas are not the name of a book. They refer to the eternal knowledge of God. Every time the Lord creates the world, He manifests the Vedas, and when He dissolves creation, He absorbs them back into Himself. Hence, the Vedas do not have an author. They are called *apauruṣheya,* meaning 'books that were not composed by anybody'.

At the beginning of creation, God revealed the eternal Vedas in the heart of the first-born Brahma, who passed them to his disciples, who further passed them to their disciples. In this way, the Vedas were transmitted orally. Thus, another name for them is *Śhruti,* meaning knowledge that was received by the tradition of hearing (listening). These were finally written down by Ved Vyas, who divided the entire body of knowledge into the four Vedas—*Ŗig Veda, Yajur Veda, Sāma Veda* and *Atharva Veda.* But Ved Vyas is never declared to be the author of the Vedas. Vyas in Sanskrit means 'compiler', and as his name suggests, Ved Vyas is the one who compiled the Vedas and classified them into four parts.

The same Vedic knowledge was further elaborated in other scriptures. These include the two *Itihās'* (Ramayan and Mahabharat), eighteen Puranas, *Ṣhaḍ Darśhan* (six treatises on philosophy), hundred *Smṛitis* (books of dharma) and thousands of *Nibandhs* (philosophical thesis by great sages). Together, this entire body of literature is referred to as the Vedic scriptures. These are the great books for acquiring divine wisdom. Even Western philosophers offer profuse admiration for them. To quote a few:

> Vedas are the most rewarding and the most elevating book which can be possible in the world.
>
> – Arthur Schopenhauer

> There is no book in the world that is so thrilling, stirring and inspiring as the Upanishads.
>
> – Max Müller

> After the conversations about Indian philosophy, some of the ideas of quantum physics that had seemed so crazy suddenly made much more sense.
>
> – W. Heisenberg

In the great books of India, an empire spoke to us, nothing small or unworthy, but large, serene, consistent, the voice of an old intelligence, which in another age and climate had pondered and thus disposed of the questions that exercise us.

– Ralph Waldo Emerson

Whenever I have read any part of the Vedas, I have felt that some unearthly and unknown light illuminated me. In the great teaching of the Vedas, there is no touch of sectarianism. It is of all ages, climes and nationalities and is the royal road for the attainment of the Great Knowledge. When I am at it, I feel that I am under the spangled heavens of a summer night.

– Henry David Thoreau

From the Vedas, we learn a practical art of surgery, medicine, music, house building under which mechanised art is included. They are an encyclopedia of every aspect of life, culture, religion, science, ethics, law, cosmology and meteorology.

– William James

India—The land of Vedas, the remarkable works contain not only religious ideas for a perfect life, but also facts which science has proved true. Electricity, radium, electronics, airship, all were known to the seers who founded the Vedas.

– Ella Wheeler Wilcox

Evidently, these wonderful scriptures contain immense knowledge. But how can we access their content? We study books for materialistic knowledge, but it usually does not suffice. We also need a teacher who can explain the complex matter contained in them. Similarly, we need a teacher in the spiritual field as well.

The Vedic scriptures are undoubtedly a treasure house of divine knowledge. Still, they are so many, and the knowledge in them is so sublime, that it is not easy to comprehend them on our own. Their complexities can easily baffle an unguided reader. Hence, the Vedas themselves instruct that they should be understood under the guidance of a guru. The *Yajur Veda* states:

tadvijñānārtham sagurumevābhigachchhet
samitpāṇih śhrotriyaṁ bhrahmaniṣhṭham

(*Muṇḍakopaniṣhad* 1.2.12)

'To know the Truth, approach a spiritual master, who is both well-versed in the theoretical knowledge of the scriptures and has realised it by practical experience.' The Shreemad Bhagavatam states:

tasmād guruṁ prapadyeta jijñāsuḥ śhreya uttamam
śhābde pare cha niṣhṇātaṁ brahmaṇy upaśhamāśhrayam

(11.3.21)

'One who is desirous of the highest welfare should surrender to a true guru. Such a guru should be both theoretically knowledgeable and practically realised.' The *Pañchadaśhī* states:

tatpādāmburu hadvandva sevā nirmala chetasām
sukhabodhāya tattvasya viveko 'yaṁ vidhīyate (1.2)

'Serve the God-realised guru with a pure mind, giving up doubts. He will then bring you great happiness by helping you develop a discriminative intellect and knowledge of the scriptures.' In this way, the Vedic scriptures advise us repeatedly about the importance of the guru on the spiritual path. The great sages state the same thing. Jagadguru Shankaracharya said:

yāvat gururna kartavyo tāvanmuktirna labhyate

'Until you surrender to a genuine guru, you cannot be liberated from material bondage.' Hence, one of the most magnanimous graces of God is when He brings the soul in contact with a true guru.

Fortunately or unfortunately, in modern times, we have access to the knowledge of numerous gurus. They seem to be presenting so many different ideas and methodologies that the listener becomes confused. How do we know which guru's interpretation is correct and which is not? Is there any way to validate whether any guru is imparting to us knowledge of the Absolute Truth and not just his personal opinion of the Truth? This can be established based on two points:

1) What the guru says should be as per the authority of the scriptures. If this is not so, then the doubt remains whether the knowledge he bestows is merely his personal viewpoint. Even if one per cent of his knowledge is fallacious, it becomes untenable.

2) What the guru says should be aligned with what the other gurus of the past said. There have been many gurus in Indian history like Soordas, Tulsidas, Meerabai, Guru Nanak, Kabirdas, Narsi Mehta, Shankaracharya,

Madhvacharya, Ramanujacharya, Nimbarkacharya, Chaitanya Mahaprabhu, Vallabhacharya, etc. If our guru teaches the same Truth that the gurus of the past did, and the same is written in the authentic Vedic scriptures, then we can confidently have faith that our guru is presenting authoritative knowledge of the Absolute Truth.

This is the triad of guru (our spiritual master), sadhu (all the other gurus in history), and śhāstras (the Vedic scriptures). When all three—guru, sadhu, and śhāstras—confirm the same principle, then we can be reassured that the knowledge we are receiving from the guru is authentic and reliable.

Thus, we must find a true guru and then learn the Absolute Truth from him. Here, we do need to bear in mind that the process of transfer of spiritual knowledge from the teacher to the student is very different from that of material knowledge. Conventional education does not require deep respect for the teacher. The transmission of knowledge is typically purchased by paying the teacher's fees. But spiritual enlightenment is not imparted to the student by a mechanical teaching process; nor is it purchased for a price. It is revealed in the heart of the disciple by the guru's grace when the disciple develops humility, and the guru is pleased with the service attitude of the disciple. Hence, the Bhagavad Gita states:

tad viddhi praṇipātena paripraśhnena sevayā
upadekṣhyanti te jñānaṁ jñāninas tattva-darśhinaḥ (4.34)

'Learn the Truth by approaching a spiritual master. Inquire from him with reverence and render service unto him. Such an enlightened saint can impart knowledge unto you because he has seen the Truth.'

In the above verse, Lord Krishna says three things for the transmission of divine knowledge: 1) Approach a spiritual master. 2) Inquire from him submissively. 3) Render service to him.

Along the same lines, the great king Prahlad said:

naiṣāṁ matis tāvad urukramāṅghriṁ
  spṛiśhatyanarthāpagamo yadarthaḥ
mahīyasāṁ pāda rajo 'bhiṣhekaṁ
  niṣhkiñchanānāṁ na vṛiṇīta yāvat

(Shreemad Bhagavatam 7.5.32)

'Until we bathe ourselves in the dust of the lotus feet of a saint, we can never experience the transcendental platform.'

Thus, the verdict of the scriptures is that we need to find a true guru and surrender to him to receive divine knowledge of the scriptures. But what if we have not yet found a guru? Should we wait for one before we proceed further on the path? No, we must not wait. We should keep progressing on the path of self-unfoldment with the help of whatever knowledge we have gathered. By the grace of God, we will find our guru later along the journey.

Conclusion

In this chapter, we discussed how success in life requires cultivating both kinds of knowledge—material science for the upkeep of our physical requirements and spiritual wisdom for the manifestation of our inner divinity. We saw how, in the material field, even one piece of information could make such a huge difference to our craft, our business and our health. We also discussed how, in the spiritual realm, knowledge has various utilities. It helps us understand the Absolute Truth. It enables us to understand our relationship with God. And it shows us the proper technique for devotion and sadhana.

But mere knowledge of the techniques does not suffice either. Their implementation requires self-control, abstinence and self-abnegation. This is where the attitude of discipline comes in. In the next chapter, let us learn how to implement knowledge through the mindset of 'discipline'.

CHAPTER 6

THE MINDSET OF DISCIPLINE

We discussed the mindset of knowledge, which provides us with information about the techniques and methodologies for success, happiness and fulfilment. By cultivating this mindset, we get the gems of wisdom that make the vital difference in our life. However, mere knowledge is also not enough. Its application requires discipline and self-control.

There are so many knowledgeable scholars whose lives are as soiled as dust rags. When it comes to living the noble virtues, their learning amounts to nought. Why is this so? Because they fail to implement their stockpile of knowledge in real-life situations and behaviours. Thus, after knowledge, we now need the sixth mindset for success, and that is the virtue of discipline.

If there is one magic word that stands out above all the rest in enriching the quality of our lives, it is discipline. We may possess the knowledge of all the libraries of the world in our head, but we will not benefit from it without the willpower to implement it.

Discipline is thus the bridge between intention and accomplishment, between inspiration and achievement, between knowledge and practice. It empowers us to do the right thing even though it may be difficult. Likewise, it enables us to desist from engaging in detrimental activities though they may seem to be pleasurable.

The Correlation between Self-control and Success

Most personal and social problems centre around our lack of self-control. Underachievement at school, procrastination at work, alcoholism, drug abuse, lack of exercise, unhealthy diet, rude behaviour, explosive anger, etc. are all connected to poor self-control. In fact, lack of willpower correlates to almost every kind of iniquity, such as addiction, vices, an uncontrolled tongue, lethargy and sloth.

On the other hand, abundance of willpower enables us to practise discipline in life. It provides us with the strength to resist temptations and shun fleeting attractions. Those who have self-control possess the ability to restrain the turbulent senses from tripping every time there is an allurement in the environment. They are also able to prevent the mind from running helter-skelter. They keep a razor-sharp focus upon the task at hand and accomplish brilliant results.

Several studies have been conducted by social scientists to isolate the personality traits that contribute most to success in any field of human endeavour. Of the many characteristics that prove helpful, such as positivity, responsibility, inspiration, etc., research has shown that the two qualities having the biggest correlation to accomplishment are 'intelligence' and 'self-control'. Those who rank higher on both intelligence and self-control have a greater chance of succeeding in any field of human endeavour.

Now, intelligence is mostly innate. We have a given level of intellect, and there is only so much we can do to enhance it. However, self-control, i.e. willpower, is very much in our hands, and it can easily be increased or decreased by our thoughts and actions.

Unfortunately, most people perceive they fall short on this essential prerequisite for success. When asked about their strengths, they name kindness, humour, bravery, honesty and even humility, but not self-control. In surveys conducted by researchers, people were asked to identify their strong points from a list. Self-control was the least selected. Conversely, when they were asked to choose their failings, lack of willpower was the most widely picked. It thus topped the list of weaknesses.

This widespread shortcoming in human nature has been further exacerbated in modern times by easy accessibility to temptations. A few centuries ago, there were no research psychologists. Consequently, we have no way of knowing the extent to which desires tormented our ancestors in the medieval times. However, we do know that 90 per cent of the population lived in villages and was engaged in farming. When they returned from a hard day's work in the fields, they did not have many options for indulging their senses. There were no media blitzes, box office busters or luring internet sites. There were very few temptations besides smoking hookah, drinking alcohol, indulging in sexual gratification and sleeping.

The situation has radically changed in today's age of smartphones, television, movies, the internet and casinos. These have dramatically increased the challenges of maintaining self-control. People feel even more vulnerable because temptations are usually available at an arm's length. Even at work, the mind can escape the drudgery of the office in a moment. With the click of a mouse, you can be off surfing the World Wide Web, or with the ever-present mobile, you can be chatting and texting with friends and relatives. The tedious work at hand can very easily be put off by visiting Facebook, viewing YouTube, surfing gossip sites or playing video games.

In this situation, most people realise they need more willpower to focus their mind, manage their emotions and control their senses. Yet, they are unable to get their act together before the growing temptations luring them. Most people sincerely believe more self-control would benefit their professional career, physical health and interpersonal relationships. Nevertheless, from time to time, they feel like willpower failures. According to the American Psychological Association, Americans name lack of willpower as the number one reason they struggle to reach their goals.

To understand the extent to which people battle with desire, Roger Baumeister, a German social researcher, conducted an experiment on more than two hundred men and women, in central Germany. He handed them electronic gadgets that would beep randomly during the day. When the beepers went off, folks were to note whether they were experiencing desire. The conclusion of the study was that about half the time people were feeling some desire, and another quarter of the time they had experienced a desire just a few minutes back.

The most commonly experienced desire was the urge to eat. It was followed by the impulse to sleep. Then came the desire for leisure—like taking a break from work by surfing the internet instead of writing the memo. Next came sexual impulses, a little ahead of the temptation for interaction via social networking sites. After this were listening to music and watching television.

Many were desires they were consciously trying to resist. Baumeister concluded that people spend a considerable portion of their waking hours resisting desires.

How did people fare in resisting desires? Researchers found that people were reasonably strong in resisting the urge for sexual gratification. They were mediocre in passing up food and soft drinks. But when it came to television, the internet and other media attractions, they failed nearly half the time.

The above statistics reveal the widespread nature of the struggle to control the mind and senses. Those who triumph at it develop focus, avoid procrastination and stay away from wasteful activities. Those who are weak in self-control keep struggling with distractions, laziness and vices.

The Battle between the Mind and the Intellect

The struggle for self-control is a natural part of our life. As humans, we possess internal instruments consisting of the senses, mind and intellect. Amongst these, the intellect is rational and looks for value. It analyses, 'I need to work towards long-term benefits and not get distracted by immediate gratification.' But the mind and the senses rebel like little children yearning for enjoyment. They tug at the intellect, saying, 'Let us indulge in this pleasure now, irrespective of the long-term consequences. We'll deal with them later when we have to.'

Thus, while the intellect considers the value of an action, the mind and senses look for immediate pleasure. If there is enjoyment in eating the fourth jalebi, they pine for it. Of course, the temptations are different for all. The smoker craves for a cigarette, the shopaholic craves to spend, the gambler craves for a night at the casino, etc. Nevertheless, whatever the attractions that the pleasure-seeking senses and the indulgent mind seek, the intellect plays the role of reining them in through the power of reason.

Consequently, a conflict ensues. The intellect suggests a behaviour that is beneficial in the long run. The mind and senses seek to avoid pain and look for instant gratification. This is where the discerning power of the intellect is necessary. It must remain firmly anchored to the beneficial versus the pleasurable, thereby forcing the mind and senses to behave accordingly.

The Vedas have classified two kinds of happiness: *shreya* and *preya*. Śhreya is the kind of happiness that seems like bitter poison in the beginning but turns out to be like sweet nectar later. For example, to wake up early and exercise may be extremely painful to practise. But when health improves as a consequence of it, we realise that the benefits are well worth the hard work and sacrifices made.

The direct opposite is preya happiness, which is like nectar in the beginning but transforms into poison later. For example, if we feast on a large cup of chocolate chip ice cream every day, it may give us immense pleasure momentarily. But when the body's physical parameters inevitably go out of control, the initial joy turns into agonising misery.

Regarding śhreya and preya, the *Kaṭhopaniṣhad* states:

anyachchhreyo 'nyadutaiva preyasteubhe
   nānārthe puruṣhaṁ sinītaḥ
tayoḥ śhreya ādadānasya sādhu bhavati
   hīyate 'rthādya u preyo vṛiṇīte
śhreyaśhcha preyaśhcha manuṣhyameta stau
   samparītya vivinakti dhīraḥ
śhreyo hi dhīro 'bhi preyaso vṛiṇīte
   preyo mando yogakṣhemād vṛinīte   (1.2.1–2)

'There are two paths—one is 'beneficial' and the other is 'pleasant'. These two lead humans to very different ends. The pleasant is enjoyable in the beginning but it ends in pain. The ignorant are snared to the pleasant and perish. But the wise are not deceived by its attractions. They choose the beneficial and finally attain true happiness.'

The reality of life is that pleasures which pull us down and degrade the mind are usually readily available, while worthwhile pleasures invariably lie upstream. To reach them requires hard work and earnest effort. Hence, the need for discipline. The noble virtue of discipline enables us to accept the voluntary inconvenience of behaving in the manner our intellect decides as correct, despite the tugging of the mind and senses. Therefore, it is one of the principal factors for triumph in life.

The Price for Success

In recent times, several commercials offer instant success that comes packaged for a price. These advertisements urge you to buy a lottery ticket and become an instant billionaire, eat this wonder food and lose fifteen kilograms in one month, earn ten lakh rupees a year by spending two hours daily on the internet or purchase a particular face cream to wipe twenty years off your face.

Unfortunately, these claims are a far cry from the reality of life. Success and proficiency in any field require practice, hard work and a steady plod upwards. The TV commercials displaying the winner of the National Lotto jumping up and down with glee are misleading. They do not reveal information about the millions who lost. If each loser of the lottery was allowed ten seconds on TV to say, 'I purchased the lottery ticket but lost', it would take a few years for everyone to finish speaking.

To attain any measure of accomplishment in life, we must let go of our lottery-winning mindset. Waiting for the jackpot is behaving like a crackpot. Instead, we must come to terms with the fact that achieving success requires dedication, perseverance and steady effort. The English poet, H.W. Longfellow, put it well:

The heights by great men reached and kept,
Were not attained by sudden flight;
But they, while their companions slept,
Were toiling upward in the night.

In all fields of human endeavour, **practice is the key that opens the door to excellence.** A Swedish psychologist and professor at Florida State University, K. Anders Ericsson, published an insightful paper in 1993, titled *The Role of Deliberate Practice in the Acquisition of Expert Performance*. He studied world-class performers in music, sports and dance, to understand what led to their immense talent. The results debunked the theory that top-notch performers are born gifted.

In his research paper, Ericsson concluded that the difference between expert performers and normal adults reflects a life-long period of deliberate effort to improve performance in a specific domain. In addition, when one considers the prerequisite motivation necessary to engage in deliberate practice every day for years and decades, when most children and adolescents of similar age engage in play and leisure, the real constraints on the acquisition of expert performance become apparent. While the actual number of hours of practice varies and is not the only reason for success, the widely used rule of thumb is about ten thousand hours of practice as popularised by Malcom Gladwell in his famous book, *Outliers*. This means that one must practise for about three hours daily for ten years to achieve some notable measure of success.

Similarly, the key to spiritual mastery over the mind is also practice. In the Bhagavad Gita, when Shree Krishna instructed Arjun to control the mind and attach it to God, Arjun confided that it was challenging to accomplish:

chañchalaṁ hi manaḥ krishṇa pramāthi balavad dṛiḍham
tasyāhaṁ nigrahaṁ manye vāyor iva su-dushkaram

(6.34)

Arjun said, 'O Shree Krishna, the restless mind is very turbulent, strong and obstinate. It appears to me that it is more difficult to control than the wind.' To this, Lord Krishna responded:

asanshayaṁ mahā-bāho mano durnigrahaṁ chalam
abhyāsena tu kaunteya vairāgyeṇa cha grihyate   (6.35)

'O mighty-armed son of Kunti, what you say is correct; the mind is indeed tough to restrain. But by practice and detachment, it can be controlled.'
Sage Patanjali taught the same principle:

abhyāsa vairāgyābhyāṁ tannirodhaḥ
(*Patañjali Yog Darśhan* 1.12)

'The perturbations of the mind can be controlled by constant practice and detachment.'

In the above verses, *abhyās* (practice) is an important word. It means a concerted and persistent effort to change an old habitual behavioural pattern and develop a new one. Through repeated training or practice, the obstinate and turbulent mind is brought under control. Thus, mastery in the spiritual and material realms comes at a price. Here is a simple story to illustrate the same point:

A king wished to leave behind the essence of wisdom for future generations. He asked his ministers to frame a text that would encapsulate the wisdom of the present age. The ministers took the task seriously and went to work together, reviewing books and discussing amongst themselves. Finally, they came up with a three-and-a-half page draft.

The king looked at their draft and said, 'This treatise is full of many wonderful gems of knowledge. But I feel it is too wordy. People will not have time to read it. Please shorten it.'

The ministers went back to their conference room. They reworked the draft and returned to the king with a one-page message. The king reviewed it again and responded, 'It is still too long. I want a short message that can be read in a jiffy. Please shorten it further.'

The ministers took this up as a challenge. They discussed and deliberated, and finally reduced it to just five words. When they took their aphorism of wisdom to the king, he was delighted. 'It is perfect!' he exclaimed. 'This is the wisdom to pass on to posterity.'

The five words were: THERE ARE NO FREE LUNCHES.

Nothing is free. No matter what we wish to attain, there is always a price for it. If our goal is to become proficient in a particular skill, the price for it is practice. That answer seems to be very obvious. But then why is spectacular achievement so rare? Why do many more not put in the practice required for it?

The reason is that the majority shy away from austerity, sacrifice and the pain of preparation. They would not mind a free lunch, but if they have to pay with austerity, they are not interested. Those who climb to great heights are the ones who voluntarily embrace the discomfort of practice.

Edwin Moses, a former American athlete, holds the all-time record for the maximum consecutive victories in a track event.

In the 400 metres hurdles, between 1977 and 1987, he won 122 consecutive races including 107 finals and 15 heats. He set the world record for the event four times. He won the gold medal in the 1976 and 1984 Olympics. He could not compete in the 1980 Olympics because of the US boycott of the Moscow Olympics.

Moses was elected as the first chairman of the Laureus World Sports Academy, which honours individuals and teams for outstanding achievement in sports throughout the year. With a mission to use the power of sports to change the world, these awards support over one hundred community projects in about forty countries. Journalists once asked him about the secret of his success. He responded by saying, 'I have a greater ability to tolerate pain than others.'

Moses' testimonial is very educative. Proficiency has to be built on the bedrock of hard work.

Willingness to tolerate discomfort is thus the universal prerequisite for success. In the book, *The New Common Denominator of Success*, the author Albert E.N. Gray says that he stumbled on the most important realisation in his life. He writes that those who succeed have the habit of doing things that failures do not like to do. Successful people do not like doing them either, but they subordinate their dislike to the strength of their purpose.

Gray's words were validated by a study done on a typical American factory. It was observed that, on an average, a production line worker watched thirty hours of television a week. The production line supervisor viewed television twenty-five hours a week, while the foreman watched twenty hours. Only twelve to fifteen hours were spent by the plant superintendent. The company president sat in front of the TV even less, about eight to ten hours a week. Finally, the chairman of the board watched only four to eight hours of TV every week, and of that, 50 per cent were training videos.

The trend in the figures above speaks for itself. Greater self-control is undeniably correlated to the height to which one rises in professional life.

Having established the value of discipline, let us now take a peek at how it evolves in life, beginning with childhood. Hopefully, this will give us an inkling into the secrets of enhancing willpower in ourselves.

The Importance of Self-control from Childhood

In the African savannah, when the mama giraffe gives birth to its calf, she does not sit on the ground for the delivery. Instead, she stands on her tall legs and the baby falls to the ground from a height of eight to nine feet. The poor calf is pained by the fall and curls up on the hard earth.

But the mama's heart does not melt on seeing the pain of her child. She kicks her baby with her hard hooves. The infant calf cringes in agony and, rolling over on the ground, it gets up. Mama giraffe still does not relent. She kicks her baby again and knocks it to the ground, forcing the calf to learn to get up on its feet.

This harsh behaviour by the mother giraffe may seem extremely cruel to us. But the mother knows that the child has only a few minutes to learn to walk before the lions come. There is simply no time for indulgence. There is no time to enjoy the bliss of curling up on the ground. The child learns to ignore the pain for the sake of survival.

We often underestimate the importance of self-control in children. However, a researcher from Stanford, Walter Mischel, conducted a famous experiment to study the self-control of toddlers. The trial was named 'Marshmallow Test'.

The test observed how much children could postpone immediate gratification for a more significant long-term reward. Since very long-term rewards do not attract them, the test was ingeniously designed to measure their self-discipline in the short run.

The toddlers were placed in solitary rooms with a marshmallow in front of them. They were told that if they did not eat it for twenty minutes, they would receive an extra marshmallow at the end, and thus enjoy double. Their behaviour was then observed from outside.

Some children, having no thought for restraint, ate the marshmallow right away. Others dallied for a while, but finally succumbed to the temptation and had the marshmallow. It was interesting to observe the strategies they adopted to resist the temptation at hand. Some squirmed and looked away, deliberately avoiding the marshmallow, but finally caved in. Obviously, willpower was in short supply and the children struggled with delayed gratification. Only a few children held out for twenty minutes to receive the reward at the end.

Initially, nobody suspected the strong correlation between the toddler's willpower and their future success. However, the research study got an interesting twist many years later. Walter Mischel's daughters had been among the toddlers tested at Bing Nursery School. They later studied at Stanford, where some of their colleagues had also been a part of the test. At that point, interest in the experimental data was revived. The research records were revisited to see how well the children fared as they grew up and they were further observed for another ten years. In this manner, the lives of the children were observed over three decades.

The study revealed that children who had resisted the marshmallow for a full twenty minutes were faring better in every sphere. The virtue of self-control helped them in all realms, as it enabled them to delay immediate gratification for long-term gain. They had better academic grades; they did better in their careers; they had harmonious relationships; they were less addicted to alcohol and drugs; they were healthier and happier; they did not have any criminal convictions.

The children who managed to hold on for the entire twenty minutes went on to score an average of 210 points higher on the SAT scores than the ones who succumbed in the first minute. Those with greater willpower were more popular amongst their peers and teachers due to better control over their moods. They earned higher salaries. They had a lower body mass index (BMI) and virtually no instance of drug abuse. The correlation between willpower and success was astonishing.

On the other hand, children with the weakest self-control had a 40 per cent record of criminal conviction. They worked in low-paying jobs and had little money in their account. They were less likely to own a home or have money set aside for retirement.

The above study by Walter Mischel, which was graphically called 'Toddlers' Torture', amply highlights the correlation between willpower and success in life. But is it possible to increase the willpower of children right from infancy? It is, as opined by Dr Richard Ferber.

The Technique of Ferberisation

Most of us have heard of vulcanisation of automobile tires. We have also heard of galvanisation of steel. But what in the world is 'Ferberisation'? It is a technique applied to increase the self-control of infants who are above six months old.

Whenever babies feel distressed, it is natural for them to cry. The immediate response of parents is to rush to their comfort and try to quieten them. Dr Richard Ferber, director of the Pediatric Sleep Disorders Center at Boston Children's Hospital, says this natural reflex action by parents sends a wrong message to infants. They learn that crying is helpful because it brings assistance from adults. But it prevents children from developing the strength to handle issues by themselves.

Dr Ferber advises parents to control the natural urge to rush to their baby's help every time it cries. Instead, he recommends that the baby be allowed to learn to cope with its issues. He says that you can go to it after a few minutes and reassure the baby that you are there, but do not lift and hug it. He also suggests a detailed chart of the intervals at which you should visit and comfort the baby. This time interval should be progressively increased as the days go by.

What are the benefits of such training? Jodi Mindell studied the benefits of Ferberisation in 2006. She found that it led to the following positive outcomes:

- Children who complete sleep training are less likely to throw bedtime tantrums.
- Children who have been Ferberised are more likely to settle down at night within ten minutes.
- Children who complete the training are less likely to awaken their parents during the night.
- Parents who Ferberise their babies report improvements in their stress levels, mood and interactions with their children.

In addition to these positive results, parents reported improvements in their children's daytime behaviour, perhaps because the little ones, who had now become sleep training 'graduates', were getting more sleep at night.

It is interesting to note that, through Ferberisation, even infants can be taught the art of self-control. Long before children can read rules or perform chores, they can flex and develop their willpower muscles!

However, what should we do if we were not Ferberised in childhood? Are there techniques that we can resort to as grown-ups to increase our reservoir of willpower? There definitely are, but first this requires a deeper understanding of the nature of willpower.

Let us try to understand the source of willpower in the human body. Hopefully, that will give us an inkling into its secrets.

The Willpower Muscle

Amongst all mammals, humans have the largest brain in proportion to their body weight. The human brain makes up one-fortieth of the body mass. More significantly, it consumes a staggering one-fifth of the calories we burn for energy. Even more importantly, the human brain has a very large prefrontal cortex, a lobe of the brain right behind the forehead and eyes.

The main task of the prefrontal cortex in the human brain is to enable us to do the harder thing and to forsake the more pleasurable one. When it is easier to continue lying in bed in the morning, the prefrontal cortex empowers us to get up and go about our daily chores. When it is more comfortable to sit and watch television from our living room, it enables us to avoid being a couch potato and go for yoga practice. Thus, **the prefrontal cortex is central to what makes us human. It provides us with willpower and self-control.** Interestingly, even within the brain, the prefrontal cortex consumes a surprisingly large portion of energy. This has been validated by measuring the glucose level in a person's bloodstream, before and after performing a self-control task. It is observed that after exerting one's willpower, the glucose level drops substantially.

Willpower has three aspects to it:

1) **I want:** What are the long-term goals that we should keep at the back of our mind and focus our energies on?

2) **I will:** If there is something that will improve the quality of our life, we need to do it even though it is tedious and painstaking.

3) **I won't:** If we have a habit that undermines our health and happiness, we need to stop doing it though it may be pleasurable.

The prefrontal cortex provides us with the three powers: 'I want', 'I will' and 'I won't'. Self-control is about harnessing these three powers that are enabled for humans by the prefrontal cortex.

Animals have negligible prefrontal cortex in proportion to their brain mass. Thus, they cannot reject the more pleasurable in favour of the more beneficial. A cow will not say, 'I enjoy green grass, but for spiritual advancement, I will practise austerities and consume dry hay.' However, humans possess vivek. Utilising that discerning intellect is what differentiates us from animals. It is said:

tattva vismaraṇāt bhekivat

'The moment humans forget wisdom, they descend to the level of animals.'

Now the questions that arise are: Is our willpower constant from morning till evening? And does it remain the same day after day? Interestingly, willpower behaves very much like a mental muscle. It gets fatigued when it is used. If we perform a task that requires immense self-control, willpower gets depleted by the end of it. Often it does not bounce back until the next day (after sleep and renewal).

Researchers have some standard procedures for testing willpower. One such test is to ask people to solve a puzzle that is actually unsolvable. Since they do not know it is unsolvable, they keep working at it until their willpower gives way. The amount of time they work on it, before giving up, is taken as a measure of their willpower. Another test is to get people to squeeze the hand exerciser. The duration for which they continue to press it before giving up indicates the strength of their willpower.

In one willpower test, students were invited to snack. They were divided into two groups. The unlucky group was taken to a room that had raw radishes and delicious-smelling cookies. They were asked to wait in the room and eat the radishes if they chose to, but not the cookies. Their reactions were observed through a small window. They were obviously tempted and gazed longingly at the mouthwatering aromatic cookies, but then settled down to nibble at the bland radishes. The students were then taken to another room and given puzzles to work upon. They thought they were being tested for cleverness but did not know that the puzzles were, in fact, unsolvable.

The second group of students was guided to a room that had freshly baked hot cookies placed in a bowl. They were told they could eat all they wanted. Then they were given the puzzles to solve. The test in both cases was to see how long they would work on the riddles before giving up.

Interestingly, the students who had feasted upon the cookies attempted to solve the questions for an average of twenty minutes. But the unlucky group, which had been harshly tested and offered radishes, gave up in just eight minutes on an average. They had successfully exerted their self-control in resisting the cookies, but the effort had depleted their stock of willpower for the puzzles.

The conclusion from the above study was that willpower gets fatigued when exercised, very much like the physical muscles of the body. This also explains the phenomenon where someone who has been displaying exemplary self-control for a full week by going to the gym and sticking to the proper diet, suddenly finds the willpower snapping. After a week of abstinence, he/she goes on binge eating because willpower has been exhausted.

Marital therapists say that willpower fatigue is the reason behind a behavioural pattern they observe in marriages. Where both husband and wife have challenging careers, they fight over apparently trivial matters in the evening. The reason is that the long hours of work drains their reserve of self-control. When they return home, they have none left to tolerate their partner's annoying habits. Thus, marriages tend to turn sour at the same time when stress at work is high. People deplete their stock of willpower in the office, and their home front suffers the consequences.

An important corollary from the above is that our willpower is maximum in the morning. Then, as we go about coping with the challenges at work, it keeps getting exhausted. And by night-time, self-control is almost completely depleted. This is why people are most vulnerable to indulgence and vices at night.

The reverse corollary is also true. In the morning, our self-control is brimming to the full. Therefore, it is the best time to engage in challenging tasks that require immense control and focus, such as meditation, writing books, deep contemplation, etc. As the day progresses, willpower and concentration diminish.

In the morning, the brain is well-rested and recharged. This does not mean that we are out of danger of succumbing to temptations. Although we have the *capacity* to do the harder task, we also have the *desire* to do the more pleasurable task. Hence, the risk of running out of willpower always exists, whether in the morning or at night.

This leads us to an obvious question that is of interest to all of us, and we will discuss it next.

Growing Our Willpower

We have seen how the prefrontal cortex in the human brain provides us with the faculty of self-control. Are there any means of growing this faculty that is so important for success in life? Fortunately for us, there is!

Neuroscientists have now discovered what the Bhagavad Gita had stated thousands of years ago. They have found that the brain is remarkably adept at remodelling itself. If we make our brain work at mathematics every day, the portion of the brain required for mathematics starts developing. Just as a muscle develops with exercise, the relevant areas in the brain become densely connected and get packed with grey matter. Similarly, those who regularly play tennis develop the sensory-motor regions of the brain that coordinate the muscles and limbs required for tennis. In this way, players become more proficient with repeated and consistent practice.

Recently, a new branch of neurology, called neuroplasticity, has developed, which deals with the ability of the brain to refashion and remould itself. This plastic nature of the brain can be utilised to our advantage, but can be detrimental if improperly used. Those who make their brain practise negative emotions like envy, resentment, anxiety, etc. find that it becomes more resourceful in producing negative thoughts.

Those who repeatedly harbour thoughts of drugs, alcohol or cigarettes find the brain producing further desires for them. The neural pathways of such thoughts become deeper and deeper until indulgence becomes a vice. Conversely, if we repeatedly harbour positive thoughts, those neural pathways deepen, until positive thinking becomes a habit. In this way, the neuroplastic nature of the brain allows us the scope to fashion it with practice. Five thousand years ago, Lord Krishna had revealed the neuroplastic nature of the brain when He stated:

dhyāyato viṣhayān puṁsaḥ saṅgas teṣhūpajāyate
saṅgāt sañjāyate kāmaḥ kāmāt krodho 'bhijāyate

(Bhagavad Gita 2.52)

'While contemplating the objects of the senses, one develops attachment to them. Attachment leads to desire, and from desire arises anger.'

Just as the brain's ability can be improved with practice in the fields of tennis and mathematics, it can also be enhanced in self-control. What weight training does to muscles, willpower training does to the prefrontal cortex. We can set up both kinds of willpower challenges for ourselves: 'I will' and 'I won't'. Then, by repeatedly flexing the willpower muscle, we will develop our self-control.

This is how the great saints trained their mind. Swami Ram Tirth was very attached to apples. To break that attachment, he would keep an apple in his room. Every time he passed it, he would look at it and chastise his mind. After it rotted, he would throw it away and place a fresh apple. He repeated this to enhance his willpower until the mind never troubled him on that account again.

Ramakrishna Paramahamsa wanted to insulate his mind from the lure of money. He would take *ṭaka* (money) in one hand and *māṭi* (mud) in the other. Then he would throw them up alternately, saying '*ṭaka … māṭi … ṭaka … māṭi … ṭaka … māṭi*'. That was his way of training the mind.

There is a similar story about the ancient Greek ascetic, Diogenes, who lived in a barrel outside Athens. *He would go before a statue and start imploring, 'Please give me alms … please give me alms.' Someone questioned his behaviour, saying, 'The statue cannot give you anything. Why do you waste your time begging from it?'*

Diogenes replied, 'When I go and solicit alms from the public, they will insult me. At that time, if my mind is weak, it will give up easily. But the statue cannot rebuke. So, I am strengthening my mind by practising before it.' It appears that Diogenes knew the secret of strengthening the mind through practice.

However, practice does not have to be so dramatic. It can be a simple thing like not succumbing to the urge to scratch oneself, not allowing the mind the leisure of watching television, etc. The good news is that any willpower exercise strengthens the prefrontal cortex, and this, in turn, helps in a variety of activities, such as avoiding distractions at work, keeping the mind focussed, resisting temptations of the senses, etc.

The increase in willpower is possible even by committing ourselves to any small act of self-control, such as improving the posture, avoiding sweets, refusing to succumb to peer pressure, etc. These little efforts for self-discipline help us in facing challenges that are more important like sticking to a wholesome diet or following a healthy exercise regimen.

The technique of Vipassanā is based upon the above principle. It requires the practitioner to continuously sit in one posture, from morning till evening, without moving. The body urges one to change the posture, scratch oneself or move about. But the practice entails observing the urges neutrally without reacting to them. This results in an increase of willpower, and many testify that a week's Vipassanā practice helped rid them of some troublesome vice.

However, Vipassanā is a crude and less smart way of strengthening the prefrontal cortex. A subtler and more effective method is the practice of meditation. In meditation, we aim to focus the mind while avoiding distractions. This requires the exercise of self-control to prevent the mind from being lured by distractions. Thus, in meditation, all three functions of the prefrontal cortex, 'I want', 'I will' and 'I won't' get a workout.

- In meditation, we strive to stay aware of the goal.
- We endeavour to pull the mind away from the distraction.
- We repeatedly direct the mind towards the object of meditation.

All these require the exercise of self-control. Hence, practising them during meditation results in the enhancement of grey matter in the prefrontal cortex. As a result, meditators become better not only in contemplation but also in the control of impulses, consistency of focus, awareness of goals, etc.

Research has established that an hour of meditation every day for a month changes the nature of the brain. A study revealed that as little as three hours of meditation substantially improved attention span and self-control of the practitioners. The speed at which the change takes place might seem astonishing. But it is not surprising because, just as weightlifting increases the blood flow to the biceps, meditation increases the blood flow to the prefrontal cortex.

Notably, even if our meditation is unfocussed, it still serves the purpose of developing willpower. The reason is that meditation requires us to catch ourselves from getting distracted, and then bring our thoughts back to our goal. This serves as a simulation of real-life situations where the mind urges distraction from the drudgery at work while the intellect forces it back. Meditation also helps us become more aware when the mind is distracted, so that we may bring it back to the task at hand.

Meditation is not merely a technique for spiritual attainment; it also has very practical and tangible benefits for our everyday life. It is pertinent to note that our journey to a higher goal is not so much blocked by obstacles on the path as is our getting waylaid because of easier paths towards lower goals. In this scenario, the development of the muscle of self-control serves as our insurance policy against laziness and temptations that distract us from our objectives.

The Value of Habits

In the previous section, we discussed how to enhance the vital virtue of willpower. Though we may exercise and develop it, we still have a limited inventory of it, and ultimately, it gets exhausted. We may keep a tight rein on the tongue to control what we eat. But then, one day it gives way and we find ourselves splurging on fast food and desserts. We may live frugally for many days together, restraining the desire to spend, only to spoil it all at the end by going on a shopping spree. In other words, self-control runs out after a point, and then it snaps. This brings us to the question: How do we extend our snapping point beyond the current limit?

The solution is to invest our willpower in creating beneficial habits. Compare this to living week-to-week on your paycheck versus investing a portion of your earnings for the future. The unwise spend all their income as they earn and are obliged to continue working in old age. In contrast, the wise save a bit for the future and live comfortably after retirement.

Similarly, we can either keep exerting our self-control to face the daily hour-to-hour temptations and allurements, or we can utilise a portion of our willpower to create a habit. The crowning benefit of good habits is that they convert things requiring a lot of discipline into automatic action. Once we cultivate good habits, resisting unwanted urges becomes a simple routine. Habits move things from the 'hard to accomplish' category to the 'easy to do—no thinking required' one.

What are habits? In the dictionary, one meaning of the word 'habit' is 'an outfit that a nun wears'. Similarly, we too wear our habits on our personality. The second meaning of 'habit' is an action that you do on a repeated basis with little or no effort or thought.

The benefit of habit is in the last part of the above definition. It requires little or no effort. This enables us to engage in desired thoughts and behaviour with the utmost ease. Establishing good habits thus provides an easy pathway to a healthy lifestyle, positive thinking and beneficial attitudes.

The mindsets we are discussing in this book are also habitual patterns of thought. For example, when you repeatedly respond positively to a negative circumstance, you create a habit of thinking positively, thereby improving your outlook. The result of the mindset of positivity is that no matter what happens, your mind generates happy thoughts. Similarly, the mindset of responsibility is also a habitual thought sequence we establish in our mind. Once created, our mind automatically refuses to brood over the problems, and instead, focuses upon the solutions at hand.

Bad attitudes too are created by the repetition of individual thoughts. Once they become hardened into habits, the mind generates feelings of worry, anxiety and fear, even when there is no reason to do so.

The best way to avoid bad habits is to never begin them. If you do not take that first drink, if you avoid the first cigarette, if you do not see that first pornographic movie, there is no way you can get trapped in the mesh of bad habits. However, if you have already gone down the habit lane in the wrong direction, you need to labour that much harder to get out of it. It is said that a bad habit will not go away by itself; it is an undo-it-yourself project. To learn more about habits, read my book *Art of Mind Management*.

The habits we form can be either beneficial or harmful. Compare them to computer programs. Computer programs execute the commands exactly as specified—nothing more, nothing less. They do not care whether they have been rightly or wrongly written. If a particular computer program is incorrect, the output it generates will be a mess. In the same manner, habits too can be good or bad. Bad habits create a poor character and an unpleasant life, while good habits become the foundation of a spectacular personality and a joyful life. Samuel Smiles, the Scottish author of the 19th century, put it very well when he said:

> Sow a thought, and you reap an act;
> Sow an act, and you reap a habit;
> Sow a habit, and you reap a character;
> Sow a character, and you reap a destiny.

How to Forge Good Habits

One of the biggest favours we can do to ourselves is to establish good habits of thinking and behaving. Forging a habit requires forced repetition, but once the habit is formed, the desired behaviour or thought pattern becomes easy to execute.

There are different theories regarding how long it takes to create a strong habit. The answers given by various researchers vary from as little as three weeks (twenty-one days) to approximately nine months (254 days). The period depends on the nature of the habit we wish to establish. On an average, the process of habit formation takes a little over two months (sixty-six days). Whatever be the case, it is a small austerity for the reward a good habit bestows in terms of a lifetime of peace, saving time and money, guilt release and mastery over the mind and senses. Even swans and ostriches provide forty days of warmth to their eggs to hatch them. Why, then, can we not have the patience to instil a good habit?

The Mughal emperor Akbar once asked his ministers if anyone in his kingdom could train goats to abstain from eating grass. Birbal, his wisest minister, responded, 'Badshah, I can do it, but it will require sixty days.'

'You have two months to train the goat,' said Akbar.

Birbal then proceeded to get a goat and take it home. He would place fresh succulent grass in front of the goat. But whenever it went forward to sniff and nibble it, he would smack it on the face with a stick. He continued the routine for a full two months. On the sixty-first day, he brought the goat to the court of the emperor. In one hand, he held the rope that went around the goat's neck. In the other, he had the stick.

'Is this the goat that possesses the self-restraint to refrain from eating green grass?' asked Akbar.

'Yes, oh Badshah!' replied Birbal.

Akbar instructed his servants to bring soft freshly-cut grass to him. He then placed the grass on the ground before the goat.

The goat looked at the grass. Birbal twanged the stick in the air. The goat glanced at the stick and moved back. It had learned that eating grass would result in pain.

Akbar congratulated Birbal for forging the behaviour of the unintelligent animal.

When habits can be taught to animals, then why can we humans not develop good habits and get rid of the bad ones? The problem is, creating good habits requires us to strain our willpower to the utmost. It is like a rocket that is launched into space. The rocket consumes maximum fuel during the initial period of its takeoff when it is breaking through the gravitational pull of the earth. Subsequently, when its speed reaches the escape velocity of 11.2 kilometres per second, the energy required to maintain its speed is significantly reduced.

In the same way, when we wish to break the gravitational pull of previous habits, at first we need to expend a huge amount of willpower. Then, slowly, the momentum builds up. This can be compared with the merry-go-round that children play on. Initially, when the merry-go-round is stationary, the child has to exert force to the utmost to start moving it. Then, as it picks up speed, pushing it becomes increasingly easier. Finally, the merry-go-round practically flies, moving on its own momentum. The child now jumps on to enjoy the motion. If the merry-go-round slows down, the child only places one foot on the ground to give a couple of kicks, and it again picks up speed.

Likewise, when we first begin to practise good thought or behaviour, we have to exert ourselves to the utmost. Once the momentum develops in the proper direction, it becomes easier and easier, until finally, the behaviour or attitude becomes second nature. You can tell a habit has been formed when you begin doing the work unconsciously. But unfortunately, momentum can develop on both sides. If we repeat a bad habit, it creates its own momentum that becomes hard to stop.

Whether we wish to initiate a good habit or break a bad one, we have to build up the momentum slowly. And the initial phase is the hardest—to abstain from the bad behaviour or to engage in the good one. This is the toughest part where most people lose heart and give up.

In habit creation, consistency in practice is of paramount importance. If we skip the practice, it breaks the impact of repetition. And if skipping the practice happens a few times, the habit never gets formed. This is similar to creating fire from wood. There are a few types of firewood that do not require an external flame to light them. When two pieces of such wood are rubbed against each other for some time, a fire manifests. But the condition is that they must be rubbed continuously for that long. If we rub them for a few minutes and then take a break, and keep doing the same, the wood will wear off, but the fire will not manifest. Similarly, the formation of habits requires daily practice. Skipping it even two to three times results in habit suicide. Hence, the creation of good habits requires dedication and hard work that comes from the attitude of discipline.

Conclusion

In conclusion, the mindset of discipline means doing what is right even when we do not feel like it. True freedom in life comes only when discipline becomes a way of life. In this way, the mind and the senses get trained to become subservient to the higher purpose of our intellect. Only then can we have the opportunity to be good, to do good, and to feel good.

Those who have not learnt to deny the tugging of their mind always have a problem with seeking stimulation. Their mind keeps jumping from one distraction to the next, trying to get the next quick hit of dopamine for the brain. They become addicts to the ephemeral gratification of the mind and senses, and rotate amongst various unproductive activities such as channel surfing, web browsing, drinking, chatting and the like. Or they keep relieving their mind from the drudgery of the work at hand by merely shifting focus.

Thus, the ability for deep and focussed work requires the mindset of discipline. Having reached so far in our journey towards success by tapping the power of our mindset, let us now move to the last one, which is the attitude towards the inevitable problems that arise on the path to success.

CHAPTER 7

THE MINDSET OF GROWING IN THE FACE OF PROBLEMS

No discussion on success in life can be complete without a sound strategy for handling problems. 'If anything can go wrong, it will,' the infamous Murphy's law states. When issues inevitably crop up, and they will, what mindset do we adopt towards them? Do we break down and give up, or do we leverage them as opportunities for growth and progress? Saint Kabir described very nicely how different people respond when challenged by problems:

> sonā sajjana sādhujana, ṭūṭeṅ juṛeṅ sau bāra
> durjana kumbha kumhāra ke, eke dhakā darāra

'Gold, virtuous people and the saints are resilient; you may break them a hundred times and yet they will rejoin. In contrast, evil people and clay pots are fragile; once shattered, they are broken forever.'

The distinguishing feature of the successful is not that they do not experience problems on the path. Rather, they have a mindset that enables them to remain positive in the face of adversity and even utilize the negative situation for their benefit.

In this chapter, we will discuss the attitude required for successfully negotiating obstacles and growing in the face of adversity.

Problems Are Unavoidable

One service engineer in New Delhi checked his email and found two requisitions for service. One was from a customer in Kolkata, West Bengal, complaining that the machine they had purchased had broken down and their ongoing project was in a critical state, so they wanted him to reach there the next day by the first flight. The second was a message from a factory in Kochi, Kerala, claiming that the non-functioning of the machine had resulted in the shutdown of the entire production line. He was expected to reach there by lunch the next day.

The poor engineer went to sleep, pondering how to handle both the emergencies. In the morning, when he turned on his phone, he found two voicemails demanding his visit at the earliest. One was from Cuttack, Odisha. The other was from Indore, Madhya Pradesh. On hearing the voicemails, he felt he was tottering under an unbearable weight. Nevertheless, he munched at his breakfast pensively.

After eating, he thought of checking his WhatsApp messages and found two more requisitions for his service visit: one from Rajkot, Gujarat and the other from Bengaluru, Karnataka. The service engineer picked up his briefcase, put on his coat and tie, and walked out of his house. He waved down a cab.

'Where should I take you, Sir?' asked the cabbie.

'Take me anywhere,' said the engineer. 'I don't care. I have problems everywhere.'

This is the reality of life. There are problems in all directions; nobody is exempt from them. In fact, success is sometimes defined as 'the ability to solve problems'. Those who are good at problem-solving are the most valued in every area of life. Hence, good leaders are always those who excel in their aptitude to handle difficult situations. Those who complain about aggravations at work do not realise that solving problems is the reason they have a job in the first place. A job that does not have glitches to resolve is no job at all.

Similarly, in every business venture, problems are unavoidable. All businesses are about offering solutions to the difficulties of customers. Without problems, there would be no business.

A man had gotten down from his car parked on the curbside. The car tyre had been punctured and he was replacing it with the spare one from the boot. The man's five-year-old son was sitting in the car feeling miserable about the situation. He complained to his father, 'Dad, why did this happen to us?'

'This is life, son,' replied his dad. 'This is not a TV show that we can switch the channel every time we do not like the programme.'

The father was speaking a philosophical truth of life. We can try everything in our power to avoid negative experiences, but they still hunt us down. The American cartoonist, Ashleigh

Brilliant, expressed this nicely: 'I try to take one day at a time, but sometimes several days attack me at once.'

Now, what should we do to handle difficulties and glitches we face in the work we do and the life we lead?

Expect Problems

The first point in handling impediments is, of course, to expect them. It is often not the problem that disturbs us as much as our naive expectations. When parents are blessed with a child, they assume that he will be the next Shravan Kumar—obedient and respectful—and serve them dutifully in their old age. Instead, when the son grows up to become a Rakshas Kumar —disobedient and rebellious—the parents are shocked, 'How could he become like that?'

Why did they not bear in mind from the child's birth that all outcomes were possible? Did they not look around them to see that children grow up into all kinds of individuals in the world? When things did not turn out their way, their own one-sided thinking took them by surprise and made them suffer in disappointment.

Let us be more realistic and expect problems. If we wish to climb a mountain, we naturally expect it to be uphill all the way. Similarly, if we wish to progress upwards in life, we should naturally expect to encounter adversities and hardships. Hoping that we will not have difficulties on our path because we are good is like hoping that the bull will not charge at us because we are vegan.

Prepare for Problems

When we know that there will be problems, how should we prepare for them? The best way is to anticipate them in advance and be ready to tackle them or try to prevent them even before they happen. Of course, we can only predict to a limit, and some issues will always catch us off-guard. But anticipating problems is always very helpful. Here is an anecdote on the topic:

A middle schooler sent a cryptic text message to his mother from school. 'Flunked in math. Prepare Dad.'

His mother texted him back. 'Dad is prepared. Prepare yourself.'

This is, of course, a joke, but those who anticipate problems are always at an advantage. Consider the game of chess. You will gain a competitive edge by thinking ahead. If you wish to win, you must be able to foresee your opponent's next move. Hence, you look at the options your opponent has and the scenarios that could be created by them. Similarly, in life too, you will succeed by anticipating problems before they happen, thereby becoming better prepared for them.

In boxing, the punch that knocks you out is not necessarily the hardest one; it is the one that you did not see coming. Likewise, many top-notch companies collapsed because they did not anticipate the impact of new technology that was developing in the world. Motorola is a prime example of this. At its peak, it was the biggest mobile phone manufacturing company in the world. It remained on top during the days of the

PDAs (personal digital assistants). But it could not anticipate the new technology used in iPhone and Android phones and, as a result, ran out of business. It was finally divided into many small portions and sold to various other companies.

Anticipating a problem does not mean worrying about it all the time.

I heard this joke about a husband who was woken up around 2 a.m. by his wife. 'Darling,' she said, 'I thought I heard a burglar in the living room.'

The husband stumbled out of his bed and rubbing his eyes, tottered to the living room. He found himself looking into the barrel of a revolver. The burglar made him hand over the household valuables and was about to leave.

'Before you leave,' said the man, 'I would like you to come to my bedroom and meet my wife. She has been expecting you every night for the last thirty years.'

This was a case of excessive worrying. Anticipating a problem means we evaluate the possibility of its occurrence and prepare for it.

Face the Problem

When a problem arises, what should we do? First of all, accept that we do have a problem.

Some people refuse to recognise the reality of the situation. You may have heard of the phrase, 'the elephant in the room'. It refers to an obvious problem that people are choosing not to notice. A few decades ago, a TV commercial depicted it very well. It showed a middle-class family's home. An elephant was in the room, but all the members were behaving as if they had not seen it. The father, mother, son and daughter were going about their tasks while refusing to acknowledge they had a problem at hand.

If we refuse to face an issue—like the proverbial ostrich sticking its head in the sand—it does not make the problem go away. Instead, it is counterproductive, for the issue could fester and grow bigger. On the other hand, if we acknowledge the problem and take timely remedial action, it can save us from immense botheration in the future.

In contrast to facing the problem is wishful thinking, which does not get us anywhere. The English proverb states: 'If wishes were horses, beggars would ride.' I have heard of the advertisement in a show business magazine that read: 'Lion tamer wants tamer lions.' This is an example of wishful thinking.

Thus, when a problem arises, we must acknowledge that it exists, and then devise a game plan for overcoming it. We do not need to be terrified of adversity, for it is not our greatest enemy. On the contrary, it is in facing hardships that the best human qualities tend to manifest.

Put the Problem in Its Proper Perspective

There is a huge difference between having a big problem and making a problem big. Often our mind makes mountains out of molehills. This attitudinal difference becomes strikingly visible in marriage counselling. All couples have compatibility problems. Some brush aside the differences as insignificant, while others make even tiny issues seem insurmountable.

People come to me ever so often. 'Swami-ji, I am deeply depressed.'

'What happened?' I ask.

'My spouse said harsh words to me.'

I responded once, 'Really? Your spouse spoke harshly to you, and it has depressed you. But is that sufficient reason to feel so upset? Think of the millions of soldiers who fought in the Second World War less than a century ago. How huge was their problem! They were lying in trenches, their lives endangered, with bullets flying all around. Your and my problems are insignificant in comparison to theirs.'

When we feel depressed because we have a terrible problem, we can console ourselves by thinking of those who have bigger problems. We can also reflect on how much worse our problem could have been. Then we should ask ourselves whether the problem is really as immense as we are making it out to be.

Let us learn about the proper perspective from the story of a teenage girl who went to college after graduating from school. She started living in the campus hostel, sharing a room with her roommate. Three months later, she wrote a letter to her mother:

Dear Mom,

I hate to tell you, but a month after I had started staying in the hostel, I committed a mistake. I stole fifty rupees from my roommate. With that, I rented a motorcycle. Unfortunately, while riding it, I crashed into a lamp post and fractured my leg.

But no worries, Mom. There was a handsome doctor living down the lane, who took me to his home and nursed me to health. I am happy to inform you that we have fallen in love and have decided to get married. The only problem is that there is a disease showing up in the blood test. I do hope it gets resolved before the child pops out.

And Mom, after marriage, my husband-to-be and I will be coming to stay with dad and you, because in nursing me, he lost his job. But Mom, you will not mind it. I am sure you will enjoy his company, even though he belongs to a different religion and will keep trying to convert you.

Really, Mom! None of this is true. The only thing that has happened is that I have failed in algebra. I just wanted you to see it in the proper perspective.

Very often, when problems seem to tower before us, we do not realise that it is only a matter of perspective—our mind is making mountains out of molehills. In the story above, the girl only got an 'F' in one subject. To make her mother understand that it was not the end of the world, she made her realise how much worse it could have been. Let us also see problems in their proper perspective before we feel overwhelmed by them. We can also take inspiration from little Manoj.

Manoj, a fourth grader, was of a short build; in fact, he was one of the shortest in his class. His small size made him the target of ridicule at the hands of his one-and-a-half foot taller class bully.

One day, when his father returned home, he saw Manoj looking at the street through the big end of the telescope. 'You are seeing through the wrong end,' said the father.

'No, Dad,' replied Manoj. *'My class bully is standing in the street below. I want to see him in the proper perspective.'*

That is the attitude to adopt towards problems if they seem too big. Remember that **inner strength is the biggest asset we have in the face of challenges, and a proper mindset wins half the battle.** Keeping that in mind, let us not overrate the seriousness of the difficulty at hand, and let us not underestimate our inner resources in confronting it.

Embrace the Value of Hardships

Difficulties and obstacles have a positive side to them. It is in facing them that we grow from within. A gem gets polished with friction. The finest steel is produced by putting it in fire. Similarly, the more hardships we face, the stronger we become. It does not mean that we invite adversities into our life, but if they do come, as they inevitably will, we see them as opportunities for growth. As the quote by Franklin D. Roosevelt goes: 'A smooth sea never made a skilled sailor.'

The first instinct of people when difficult situations hit them is to hate them. But obstacles are also occasions to improve ourselves from within. **The fact is that adversities have opportunities inherent in them, and opportunities do not come without problems.** Both of these go hand in hand. If we can have faith in this axiom, it will help us face obstacles positively and progress rapidly.

We can learn the benefit of hardships from this very compelling story:

Eight-year-old Akshay recently read about the lifecycle of a butterfly, in his science class. He learnt that caterpillars weave a cocoon around themselves, hibernate in it and then emerge as beautiful butterflies.

One day, Akshay was walking through his driveway, when he saw a cocoon hanging from the rose bush in his garden. He was thrilled. 'I will see the miracle of nature happening before my eyes,' he thought.

Every day, while going to school and returning from it, he would check the cocoon to see if the butterfly had started emerging. Then, one day in the morning, Akshay discovered a small tear on it. He was super excited. Every hour he would go to take a look at the progress.

By late afternoon, the butterfly had started pushing its head out. Akshay was transfixed and continued to watch as the butterfly kept ripping the cocoon apart and pushing itself out. But when it had emerged halfway, it seemed to have gotten stuck. It was unable to extract itself anymore, and the cocoon was bobbing up and down with the force of the butterfly.

Akshay felt pity for the poor thing. He ran inside and brought a pair of scissors. Feeling sorry for the butterfly, he snipped the cocoon open. It was his good deed for the day and he felt satisfied at having helped the little creature.

However, when the cocoon was cut, the butterfly fell to the ground and began squirming on the earth. Akshay observed that its stomach was swollen and wings were shrivelled. He thought that this would soon be corrected—the wings would fill up and the stomach would shrink. But what he did not realise was that this would never happen now. The struggle of pulling itself out of the cocoon was necessary for the butterfly to push the fluid from its stomach to the wings. Without that struggle, the stomach would remain swollen and the wings shrivelled.

Like the butterfly, we too look for someone to snip away all our problems, without realising that it is in facing them that we progress. Problems are God's way of helping us fill our wings to prepare us for the spiritual flight ahead. They help us develop the sublime qualities—wisdom, perseverance, patience, tolerance, etc.—that are required for reaching the supreme goal of life. Without challenges in life, how will we develop these noble virtues?

Even in school, our teacher imparted knowledge to us and then took a test at the end. The test was not unnecessary cruelty meted out to us, though it may have seemed so at that time. Rather, it was intended to evaluate whether we had mastered the knowledge that we had been taught. The test was given so that we may be promoted to the next class. Similarly, hardships that come our way are tests sent by God on the journey of life. They are designed, not for stopping us, but for promoting us to progressively higher levels of inner unfoldment and growth.

Often people ask, 'Why does God allow earthquakes, tsunamis, hurricanes, cyclones and tornadoes to happen? Is He cruel and deliberately wants to torment us with hardships? Or are they beyond His control and happen against His wish?'

Since God is all-powerful, these natural calamities cannot happen without His will. If He wanted a world free of natural catastrophes, all He needed to do was tweak the physical attributes of the earth, and natural disasters would cease forever. If natural calamities happen within His dominion, it means that He has built them into the design of the earth. Why did the good Lord do something like this?

The logical answer is that God deliberately allows hardships to befall us. He does not want us to stop progressing spiritually in life. Whenever He deems it necessary, He creates challenges that force us to exert ourselves emotionally, intellectually and spiritually, so that we may grow. **The growth God is interested in is not an enhancement of our material luxuries, rather the evolution of our soul towards supreme perfection, over a continuum of lifetimes.** We find it difficult to appreciate this point because we consider growth as an increase in physical luxuries and financial assets. But for God, progress means the development of virtues and the overcoming of iniquity.

As a wise man once said:

I prayed to God for strength; He gave me difficulties to overcome that I might become strong.
I prayed to God for wisdom; He gave me problems to solve and become wise.
I prayed to God for courage; He gave me dangers to overcome that I might become courageous.
I prayed to God for patience; He placed me in situations where I was forced to wait and become patient.
I prayed to God for love; He gave me the poor and downtrodden to serve that I might develop a loving heart.
I prayed to God for favours; He gave me occasions to transform into opportunities.
I received nothing I wanted, I received everything I needed.

Keep an Attitude of Learning

In the process of growing and evolving, it is natural that we will sometimes fail. But, rather than lament it, we should learn the lessons and move on. As the Japanese say: 'Fall seven times, stand up eight.' We only need to ensure that the mistake we made last year is not the same one we make this year as well. Let us not be like the drunkard in the story below.

I once met a drunkard walking down the street with blisters on both his ears. I asked him, 'My my ... I am sorry to see the blisters on your ears. What happened?'

'My wife left her hot electric iron on,' said the drunkard. 'When the phone rang, I picked the iron up by mistake, and placed it on my ear.'

'Okay, but what about the other ear?' I enquired.

'The idiot called again!' he replied.

To err is not a catastrophe unless we refuse to learn from it. This may be hard to believe, but successful people also experience failure almost as often as unsuccessful people do. The difference is that they improve from their experiences and grow.

The former chairman and CEO of IBM, Thomas J. Watson Sr., was asked his formula for success. He said, 'If you want to increase your success rate, double your failure rate.' He meant that the more you try, the more you will fail. The more you fail, the more you will learn. The more you learn, the more you will succeed.

Thus, success lies on the far side of failure. All successful people are those who failed many times on the journey but never regarded themselves as fiascos. For example, Albert Einstein is widely recognised as the greatest scientist in modern history. But in 1895, his Munich schoolmaster wrote in his report, 'He will never amount to anything.' Wolfgang Mozart, one of the biggest musical geniuses, was told by Emperor Ferdinand that his operas were far too noisy and contained too many notes. *The Kansas City Star* newspaper fired Walt Disney because the editor felt he 'lacked imagination and had no good ideas'.

Meerabai, the great poet-saint, was a widow and was so harassed by her relatives that she had to leave her palace in Chittorgarh and live in Vrindavan. Saint Kabir was of unknown parentage and sparsely lettered, though he lived in Kashi amidst the greatest Vedic scholars. Inimical pundits tried to kill Sage Tulsidas and stole the Ramayan that he had written. Yet, all of these remarkable personalities converted the adversities in their lives into opportunities for internal advancement.

As we can see, adversity is not our biggest enemy, rather, it catalyses learning. If we face it with the proper mindset, it can work to our advantage. In fact, adversity speaks a language of its own. The tangible benefits of a problem are:

- It always gets our attention; we cannot ignore it.
- It causes us to evaluate our situation. It is an opportunity for self-discovery.

- It challenges us with failure and forces us to tap every sinew of our resource, thereby bringing out the best in us.
- It makes us internally strong. As Robert H. Schuller, an American pastor and author, said, 'Tough times do not last, but tough people do.'

The story of Steve Jobs is a fascinating case of learning in the face of privations:

Steve Jobs was born to an unwed immigrant woman. Before his birth, his mother put him up for adoption. The condition she placed was that the foster parents-to-be should be graduates. A couple was selected for the adoption.

Unfortunately, when Steve emerged into the world, he turned out to be a boy and not a girl as expected. The couple originally chosen by his mother refused to adopt him; he was again put up for adoption. After three months, another couple was selected. They were not graduates. Steve's biological mother agreed to give him to them on the condition that they would make him a graduate.

Steve's foster parents were poor, but they stuck to their word. After his schooling, they put him in Reed College, Portland, Oregon. It was a very expensive college. Not wanting to waste his parents' money, Steve dropped out of college after just a few months. He then began living in his friends' dorms. To make ends meet, he would collect soda bottles and sell them for money.

In retrospect, Steve Jobs realised that whatever happened was for the best. Since he was not obliged to fulfil the attendance requirements, he was free to drop into any class he liked. Reed College had the best calligraphy course in the US, and that was where he learned the difference between serif and sans-serif fonts. At that time, the knowledge did not have any direct relevance to his life, but later, when he developed the personal computer, Jobs utilised this knowledge to offer various options of fonts in the computer software. According to him, Windows copied what he did, so if he had not received the knowledge of fonts, Apple computers would have had just one option for fonts, and Windows would have followed suit. Steve quoted this incident of his dropping out of college as a blessing in disguise.

By the age of twenty, Jobs had begun manufacturing computers in his parents' garage. By the time he became thirty-three years old, the company had grown to annual sales of four billion dollars. But then an unexpected thing happened to him. He was thrown out of Apple Corporation. How could he have been thrown out of the very company that he had established? The reason was that they had gotten some investors onboard the corporation as directors. And due to a difference of opinion that developed, they extricated Steve Jobs.

According to Steve, it was a very public dismissal and the humiliation he felt was excruciating. He felt he had let down the legion of innovators in Silicon Valley and owed them a personal apology.

Nevertheless, after a few months, he realised that he still liked doing the same thing—creating new technology. As a result, he established the NeXT Corporation and took over Pixar Corporation from Lucas Corporation. This time, he was unencumbered by the corporate red tape and was free to innovate to his heart's content. The technology developed by NeXT at that *time is still used in part as the backbone of the present Mac. The first nine animation movies created by Pixar fetched a staggering $7.2 billion in revenue.*

Steve Jobs quoted this episode as another blessing in disguise. Had it not been for his extrication from Apple, he would not have had the freedom to innovate the new technologies that made him so successful. Later, Apple took over NeXT and Steve returned to his original company. He was a wonderful example of someone who turned adversity into opportunity and blossomed in the face of it.

Most of us have been taught that mistakes are bad. That is correct if the mistakes have been made deliberately. But in the process of learning, unintended mistakes are natural. Think of when you first made the mistake of touching a hot stove. From this incident, you learnt that if you touch something hot, you get burnt. So, the mistake turned out to be not so bad after all, because it facilitated the learning process.

Bear in mind that if mistakes become opportunities for learning, they are not harmful. As Edwin Louis Cole, a famous American preacher and author, said, 'You don't drown by falling in the water; you drown by staying there.'

In history, there are innumerable examples of scientists who made mistakes that led them to big discoveries. It was in the year 1839 that Charles Goodyear was conducting experiments with rubber. People had given up on rubber because it melted in summer and became bone-hard in winter when frozen. But Goodyear was confident that he could find a solution to this problem. One day, Goodyear accidentally spilt rubber mixed with sulfur onto a kitchen stove. The heat transformed the rubber sap, making it soft and flexible. Subsequently, it did not become brittle even with the cold air. The accident led Goodyear to discover the process of vulcanisation of rubber that is used in so many industries today.

Some people do not venture out of their comfort zone for the fear of making mistakes. For instance, a student might think, 'I am scared of making mistakes. I will take the minimum number of courses possible in college.' The problem is that people who are scared of making mistakes do not attempt anything new. Thus, they shy away from the unknown and from challenges, which, in fact, is the biggest mistake. Take inspiration from the following piece of information:

One correspondent interviewed many successful people and discovered that almost every one of them had achieved their success one step beyond what appeared to be their biggest failure. When the outward signs indicated that there was no hope for success any longer, they were actually closest to the breakthrough needed to reach their goal. It was as if God was giving them one final test before allowing them to reach their destination.

The fact is that failure is far more common than success. There are always losses in life. Some are huge and some are tiny. For some people, a loss means the end of the world—it affects their mental health. But what distinguishes successful people from unsuccessful ones is their capacity to handle the loss and deal with disappointment. The increase in suicides, alcoholism and nervous breakdowns in modern times is proof that people have not learnt to deal with failure. Hence, if we wish to succeed, we should train for losses.

Ultimately, failure and success are both inbuilt into the journey of life. If we succeed, we will find victory, acceptance and pleasure. And if we fail, we will encounter bouts of failure, which will be accompanied by privation, pain and rejection. Now, in the journey to success, we will naturally meet with failure as well. The only way to avoid it is to stand still in life. Then we will be free from much pain and rejection. But then we will miss out on the joy and success too.

Facing Obstacles Is the Price for Improvement

We must always remember the aphorism we learnt in the previous chapter: 'There are no free lunches.' If there is a tough decision to be made, we have two alternatives: either play now and pay later, or pay now and play later. But pay we will have to, and the longer we wait, the more we will have to pay.

If we wish to improve at anything, we have to be prepared for dangers to surmount, obstacles to overcome, hardships to face and pain to bear. That is the price we have to pay for improving ourselves.

Hardships are times for practising austerity; for denying our mind and senses the comfort and luxury they demand. Often old people complain to me about all the pain and bodily discomfort they experience. Of course, I wholeheartedly sympathise with them for their woes. I give them the best advice for health and happiness that I can, based on *Yoga for the Body, Mind & Soul* and the *Science of Healthy Diet,* two books I have authored. But

242

I also remind them that old age is an unavoidable fact of life, and it must be faced. Just like them, I too will grow old one day. How can we be prepared for such situations?

See the inevitable hardship as an opportunity to practise austerity. Take it in a positive light as a *tapasyā* (voluntary privation) for spiritual upliftment. In the olden days, people would retire to the forests, mountains and caves for tapasyā in pursuit of enlightenment. We do no such thing in our life. Adopting the thought that God puts us in a situation where we are obliged to perform austerity in old age is one way to come to terms with it. With this attitude, the inevitable pain will serve to lift us up.

The eagle can teach us a few lessons on this. When a storm begins, it does not cower down before it. It flies to a high spot and waits for the wind to blow over. When the storm sets in, the eagle spreads its wings and uses the draft of wind to rise higher and higher in the sky. It does not run away from the storm, rather, it uses the storm to its advantage. While the storm rages below, the eagle soars above it.

Similarly, when the storms of life hit us and we experience failure, tragedy and disappointment, we do not need to turn around and bolt. Instead, facing the hardships gracefully allows us to rise above them.

Often, little birds like the crow get after the eagle, pestering it with their short turns and quick movements. Sometimes they even dive bomb the eagle from behind. The eagle refuses to fight with them. It simply lifts itself to such a height where the crows cannot reach it. Rather than bothering about rejoinders to pesky crows, it knows the secret of increasing its altitude, until the crows are left behind.

We can also be inspired to do the same when people pester us. Advance ahead so much that you leave them behind.

In conclusion, the most important point while facing hardships is proper attitude. The British poet, Rudyard Kipling, expressed the proper attitude towards negative situations very nicely in his famous poem 'If'. An excerpt of its interesting lines is given below:

If you can dream—and not make dreams your master;
If you can think—and not make thoughts your aim;
If you can meet with Triumph and Disaster
And treat those two impostors just the same;

If you can keep your head when all about you
Are losing theirs and blaming it on you,
If you can trust yourself when all men doubt you,
But make allowance for their doubting too;

If you can force your heart and nerve and sinew
To serve your turn long after they are gone,
And so hold on when there is nothing in you
Except the Will which says to them: 'Hold on!'

If you can fill the unforgiving minute
With sixty seconds' worth of distance run,
Yours is the Earth and everything that's in it,
And—which is more—you'll be a Man, my son!

The poem beautifully expresses the proper attitude towards adversities. Now, let us discuss how to see the grace of God in the face of hardships.

See the Grace of God in Adversity

The *Nārad Bhakti Darśhan* explains how to mould our attitude so that we may be able to keep our mind in God irrespective of the circumstances. It states:

loka-hānau cintā na kāryā niveditātma-loka-vedatvāt

(Śutra 61)

'When worldly losses happen, do not become anxious; see in them the grace of God.'

For example, let us say that a tragedy took place three years ago—a family member passed away, or there was a theft at home or the business took a downturn. Now, that event took place in the past. But if we continue to brood over it, then our mind will also be in the past. As a result, the devotional contemplation we should be cultivating in the present will cease.

yugapat jñānānupāt manaso liṅgam

'The mind is such a vessel that you can attach it to only one place at a time.' If we lament over the past, it is unavoidable that we will lose our divine consciousness towards the present moment.

What is the solution? Sage Narad instructs us to see an embedded blessing in that past setback. Look at it as an opportunity to become detached from worldly entanglement. Examples of such positive thinking could be:

- 'I was too attached to my relatives. By taking my dear one away, God taught me that all these relationships are temporary, and that I should love God instead.'
- 'I was running madly after worldly happiness. But the ill health has come as a reminder that there is no perfect happiness here, and I must pursue spiritual treasures.'
- 'The business reversal has taught me not to take life too seriously. Rather, I must learn to focus on higher and more permanent aims—spiritual goals—in life.'

Thus, by looking at setbacks as a form of grace, we can free our mind from lamentation.

Never Hold a Grudge

If someone hurts us, it is natural to feel resentment towards that person. But the problem is that in bitterness, the mind gets fixated with negativity towards the object of hatred. As it has been said: 'Resentment is like taking poison and waiting for the other person to die.' When we nurse a grudge, it dirties our mind and poisons the consciousness. Therefore, all the religions of the world promote the virtue of forgiveness. Jesus' statement on the cross is very famous:

> Father, forgive them, for they do not know what they are doing. (Luke 23:34)

What is the way for overcoming resentment? We must first understand that this material world is inhabited by materially conditioned souls. Since they are under the dominion of maya (God's material energy), they are full of material imperfections.

Thus, for their self-interest, people will sometimes hurt or even cheat us. We should not be surprised when this happens. But the trick is to see the hurt as a blessing in disguise, by thinking along the following lines:

- 'In worldly attachment, I had forgotten the goal of life. The emotional hurt I have received is an eye-opener about the real nature of the world.'

- 'I was too attached to him/her. Now that he/she cheated me, I have understood that everyone is selfish in this world. God alone loves me selflessly and is my true relative.'

- 'This person repeatedly tries to provoke me. But I will retain my peace of mind. I will see his/her provocations as tests created by God to help me master the virtues of tolerance, forgiveness and patience.'

In this way, bringing such thoughts to the mind helps us gain spiritual benefit from the adverse behaviour of others. For example:

A mahatma (saintly person) came to a place of pilgrimage and spent the night in a dharmaśālā *(free hotel opened by charitable people in India). Unfortunately, the dharmaśālā was full of mosquitoes, and at night they made mincemeat of him.*

When the mahatma realised that there was no way he could sleep, he thought, 'Even the mosquitoes in this place are benefactors. They are coaching me to spend my night in sadhana, not in sleep.'

Now, there was no solution to the mosquito bites, because the mahatma had no option but to spend the night at the dharmaśālā. By thinking positively, he was able to keep his consciousness high. Instead, he could have thought negatively, 'How terrible! What do the cleaners do? Why does the dharmaśālā manager not get this room sprayed with mosquito repellent?' By thinking in this manner, the mosquitoes would not have stopped biting him, and his mind would have been filled with bitterness.

That is why it is said that the only thing that gets worse when you nurse it is bitterness. If we can rise above it by properly managing our attitude, we will jump ahead in our personal spiritual journey. Let me tell you a beautiful story about the benefits that accrue from not harbouring resentment:

There was a stray dog that lived in a village in the state of Uttar Pradesh, India. He had a tough life. He would scavenge for morsels outside the huts of villagers. If he managed to find something, he would satiate his hunger, but most of the time, he would be famished.

One day, a dog arrived in the village from the nearby metropolitan city of Allahabad. The city dog said to his village dog friend, 'Why are you enduring such a gruelling lifestyle here? You hardly have one square meal a day. Come with me to Allahabad. You will get a feast of rasgullas, gulab jamuns and jalebis that get thrown outside the sweet shops.'

The village dog thought it was an excellent idea. They both decided to make the journey to Allahabad together, and cover the sixty-kilometre route at an easy pace, in five days.

The next day, they started off from the village at 8 a.m. in the morning. By 6 p.m. they had covered about twelve kilometres and found themselves outside a village. They deliberated, 'We are exhausted, and this village is suitable for resting. Let us spend the night here, and make some arrangement for our meal.'

However, when they were about to enter the village, the dogs of that village came barking and chased them away. There were many of them. These two dogs mulled over the problem, 'The dogs in this village are very bad. They will not let us stay here. That halt at twenty-four kilometres we had planned for the second night ... let us proceed till there.'

They continued on their journey, and around 4 a.m., they reached the second village. But there too, the dogs chased them away. Unfortunately, all dogs consider themselves the kings of their respective territories. If an outsider dog enters, they roar at them like a lion.

These two discussed, 'The dogs here are also bad. Let us continue to the next halt.' The consequence was that the five-day journey was completed in just two days because the village dogs did not let these two rest. Moreover, they did not fight with any of the dogs on the way, saying, 'Aaay ... what do you think of yourself? Let me teach you a lesson.' If they had behaved in that manner, they would have got wounded and would have been unable to complete the journey.

Likewise, there will always be people who will obstruct our way. They will oppose us and try to stop us. If we unnecessarily argue with them or resent them, we will be the losers more than anyone else. Our mind will become dirty with hatred, anger and irritation. Instead, if we develop the right attitude, we can convert the unavoidable opposition into opportunity for growth from within.

Learn to Handle Critics

While discussing the attitude towards opponents, it is apt to also touch on the topic of critics, for they too are a part of life. Statistics gathered by researches reveal:

- 25 per cent of the people you meet will not like you.
- 25 per cent will not like you, but they can be persuaded to.
- 25 per cent of the people you meet will like you, but they can be persuaded not to.
- 25 per cent of the people will like you and stand by you no matter what others say.

These statistics should free us from the anxiety of acceptance. Simply come to terms with the fact that no matter what you do, some people will not like you. Then, why waste energy trying to win them over? You can do all possible placatory antics—praise them, sympathise with them, offer them gifts—but they will still never like you.

Everyone has the right to say what they want, as long as it does not break the rules. We also have the right not to feel bad about it. They have the right to their opinion, and we have the right to disregard it. What people say and think about us does not define who we are. Their views are not what decides our self-worth. It is best to let them deflect off us like water rolls off a lotus leaf.

We have to come to terms with the fact that some people will spill garbage upon us. That is because they are themselves full of anger, frustration, anxiety and disappointment. When that garbage heaps up within them, they look for some place to dump it. So, if they happen to dump it on you, do not take it as a personal affront. Just wish them well and move on, as the story below illustrates:

Once, a dozen frogs entered a competition to reach the top of a nearby tower. A big crowd of people gathered to see the race and cheer the contestants.

The race began, and practically nobody believed that any of the frogs could reach the top of the tower. They kept screaming comments like:

'Impossible!'

'They do NOT stand a chance.'

'They are destined to FAIL.'

The frogs began collapsing one after another. But some continued to climb. The crowd continued to yell:

'They will NEVER make it.'

'The tower is too HIGH, and the slope too STEEP.'

More frogs got exhausted and gave up.

In the end, all the frogs had given up. But one frog would just not give up. He continued climbing higher and higher, and even higher. Finally, with one big leap, he scaled the top of the tower.

The other frogs were curious to know the secret of this frog's success. They asked, 'How did you manage to keep climbing, though all the onlookers were cajoling you to give up?'

That was when they came to know that this frog was stone deaf. He did not realise the crowd had been passing negative comments. He thought that they were praising him.

The wisdom of this story is that when people tell you that you cannot achieve your goals, be deaf to them. If you have a dream in your heart, be positive and optimistic, even if everyone around you is negative and pessimistic. Tell yourself, 'I will put in my best efforts, and then, by God's grace, I will succeed.'

The Path to Ultimate Perfection

In conclusion, this world is the 'University of Hard Knocks'. It is naive to expect no calamities, reversals or difficulties. If we wish to succeed in life and become happy and fulfilled, then we need to develop a proper mindset towards problems as well. The proper attitude comes by looking for spiritual value in situations.

If our goal is to maximise our material comfort, then naturally we get upset with negative circumstances. But if we desire spiritual progress, we learn to see adversity as an opportunity for growth. **Bear in mind that the pain from the hardship is temporary, while the growth that comes with facing and solving it is permanent.**

Wise parents do not take away all the struggles their children face. Rather, they allow the children to be challenged and become strong in the face of difficulties. If parents never say 'No' to anything, their children grow up spoilt and pampered. They will expect the world to fulfil even their most selfish desires. Thus, good parents do not say 'Yes' to everything the child wants. They allow children to overcome obstacles on their own and become emotionally strong.

Similarly, our spiritual Father has built problems into the grand design of the world. It is within His ability to remove them all—He could do so in an instant. But that would deprive us of the opportunities to grow spiritually. I am reminded of the evolutionary story of a piece of wood:

A wooden block went to a sculptor and requested, 'Can you please make me beautiful?'

'Yes, to beautify is my job,' replied the sculptor. 'I am ready, but are you ready?'

'I am also ready,' answered the wood.

The sculptor took out his tools and began chiselling, sawing and hammering. 'Aaah ... what are you doing?' screamed the wood. 'This is so painful! Please stop.'

'If you want to become beautiful, you will have to tolerate the pain,' said the sculptor.

'Okay ... okay ... do it, but please be gentle. Chisel only a little every day.'

The sculptor began his work again. The wood kept crying, 'Stop ... stop ... enough for today. Please let me rest. You can do more tomorrow.'

The wood kept protesting, but the sculptor continued with his work. Then one day, the wooden block became a beautiful mūrti *(idol of a deity) and was established on the altar of a temple. In the end, the whole struggle was worth it.*

The lesson here is that, like the wooden block, we too are ugly from inside. We have the flaws of anger, greed, resentment, languor, etc. If we wish to shed our infirmities and develop our inner beauty, we have to give God, the Supreme Sculptor, the freedom to work upon us. Therefore, the opportunity before us is tremendous. Let us align ourselves with the grand design of God's universe and fulfil the purpose of our presence here, by rising to the ultimate perfection one step at a time, for that is the way to success, happiness and fulfilment.

SUMMARY

We had started off our discussion by learning that a mindset is the way we habitually think. It is an internal resource that is available to all. If we can simply cultivate beneficial attitudes within ourselves, they will unlock the glorious pathways to success, happiness and inner growth.

Let us recapitulate them briefly below:

1. The first mindset is *positivity*. This is the foundation of happiness, excellence at work and good health. Positivity means to harbour happy thoughts and an optimistic attitude. It develops when we nurture gratitude in our heart for all the blessings we have received from the universe.

    However, invariably, negative thoughts creep in due to various reasons. Then what do we do? This takes us to the next mindset.

2. The second mindset is of *taking responsibility for our emotions.* Here we stop playing the blame game, and instead, take ownership for the feelings we harbour. No matter what the external environment, we have the

freedom to choose our emotions. Hence, we alone are responsible for our moods and sentiments. We must not blame anyone—neither God, nor destiny, nor even time— for our emotions.

When we take responsibility for our faulty thoughts and attitudes, it ignites in us the spark to improve ourselves. Now, to keep the spark ignited at all times and move ahead with fervour, we need the next mindset.

3. The third mindset is *inspiration*. It provides the fuel that powers us to excellence. It fills us with the zeal to put in our best in whatever we do. It also enhances our inner strength to persevere and stand tall in the face of difficulties and hardships.

But mere inspiration is also not enough. Robbers and terrorists are also inspired in their work, but what they lack is good intention. Thus, the need for the next mindset.

4. The fourth mindset is *purity of intention*. It means to harbour the desire to please God with our thoughts, words and deeds. Such pure intention immediately frees us from stress, anxiety and tension. We can purify our intention through the practice of karm yog.

Karm yog requires us to attach our mind in loving devotion to God. To practise this, we need knowledge, which is cultivated through the next mindset.

5. The fifth mindset is *cultivating knowledge.* Theory always precedes practice, hence, any technique requires knowledge for its implementation. We must acquire two kinds of knowledge in life—material and spiritual. While

there are several means to acquire material knowledge, for spiritual knowledge, we must approach a God-realised saint and the revealed scriptures.

Yet, even after getting the best of knowledge, why do we fail to apply it in our life? Because of a lack of self-control. This brings us to the need for discipline.

6. The sixth mindset is *discipline*. It is the bridge between knowledge and its implementation. It empowers us to do the right thing, though it may be difficult, and prevents us from doing the wrong thing even if it seems pleasurable.

   However, no decision can be complete without a sound strategy for handling problems. This takes us to the last mindset.

7. The seventh mindset is to *grow in the face of problems*. We should look at problems as opportunities for inner growth and progress. This helps us remain positive despite the inevitable hardships in life. With a positive approach, we can turn adversities to our benefit, and utilise them for our spiritual evolution.

Equipped with these seven mindsets, we become masters of our mind. With this mental prowess as our foremost resource, we learn to unlock the treasure chest of God's grace, and make our human life a success, in accordance with His divine plan.

The seven mindsets described in this book are in a sequence that makes it easy to appreciate the need of each mindset. Their development need not be approached sequentially, rather, we will need to work on all of them simultaneously to achieve success, happiness and fulfilment.

EPILOGUE

The Law of Infinite Potential

Through the chapters of this book, we have discovered the importance of replacing mediocre patterns of thoughts, emotions and attitudes with superlative ones. The repeated practise of these ideas and thought patterns will help us develop the mindsets required for immense happiness and fulfilment in our journey of life.

I would now like to conclude this book by explaining the 'Law of Infinite Potential'. Each and every one of us is a spiritual being and not a bag of chemicals. Our soul is not made of the five material elements (earth, water, fire, air, space), like the things of this world. According to the Bhagavad Gita, all souls in existence are eternal parts of the Supreme Soul. Hence, we are all divine, like God Himself. Isn't that amazing and wonderful?

As tiny parts of God, our potential for growth is also infinite, because our source is infinite in every way. A drop of water reflects the qualities of the ocean even though it is a very tiny part of it. A spark of fire possesses the qualities of the fire from which it has emanated. Similarly, our soul is *sat-chit-anand,* i.e. possessing eternality, knowledge and bliss, like God Himself.

Stand before the ocean and see how humbled you feel before its vastness. The earth is even bigger, with its five oceans and seven continents. But in comparison to the solar system, the earth is only a tiny dot. Like the sun, there are about four hundred billion stars in the Milky Way (science has upped these estimates since my previous books). However, the Milky Way is not the only galaxy. Like it, there are about two hundred billion galaxies in the universe.

But these mindboggling astronomical calculations do not end here. According to the Vedas, the universe we live in is one of the smallest among the innumerable universes in existence. Each universe has one Brahma, one Vishnu and one Shiv. That is the enormity of creation and its Creator. Therefore, the Vedas have named God as *Anant,* or One who is without any beginning or end.

The Infinite God is bountiful in every aspect of His creation. Can you imagine Him saying, 'I have run out of resources and cannot produce any more sunlight for the earthlings now'? Is it possible that He will ever say, 'I have run out of oxygen now. I am just too tired to create this element anymore'? Both these scenarios are impossible to conceive. Hence, His grace is also unlimited.

It is from such unlimited abundance that we all have emerged. If we find ourselves perceiving some kind of lack or scarcity in our lives, it is not because of a shortage in divine grace, but because we have not qualified ourselves to receive it. The Vedas inform us that our Eternal Father is not miserly. He has preserved for us the immense treasures of divine love, knowledge and bliss, which are ours to claim the day we become eligible for them.

The purpose of the evolutionary journey of the soul over infinite lifetimes is not to remain down in the dumps, but to rise to the highest standard of perfection set for us by God. Hence, the Law of Infinite Potential states that each one of us has endless potential for growth.

Lack of awareness of this law creates in us the scarcity mentality, which leads us to compete with each other to become 'king of the hill'. With such an attitude, we assume that there is only one hill and we all have to vie for it. But God has innumerable hills in His dominion, and He can create countless new ones if He so wishes. Hence, the only person we really need to compete with is ourselves. Our topmost priority should be to become the best person we can be and make our journey of life a success.

This book is a humble attempt to help you get in touch with your own inner resources. My aim in writing it is to make you aware of how faulty attitudes in the past may have hindered you from rising to your glory. And how replacing these with beneficial mindsets can help you find infinite abundance that God has in store for you. If the wisdom in this book contributes even a little in enriching your life's journey, I will consider my effort worthwhile.

GUIDE TO HINDI PRONUNCIATION

a	as *u* in b*u*t
ā	as *a* in f*a*r
i	as *i* in p*i*n
ī	as *i* in mach*i*ne
u	as *u* in p*u*sh
ū	as *o* in m*o*ve
e	as *a* in ev*a*de
ai	as *a* in m*a*t; sometimes as *ai* in *ai*sle with the only difference that *a* should be pronounced as *u* in b*u*t, not as *a* in f*a*r
o	as *o* in g*o*
au	as *o* in p*o*t, or as *aw* in s*aw*
ṛi	as *ri* in K*ri*shna
ḥ	it is a strong aspirate; also lengthens the preceding vowel and occurs only at the end of a word. It is pronounced as a final *h* sound

ṁ	nasalises and lengthens the preceding vowel and is pronounced as *n* in the French word Bo*n*.
ka	as *k* in *k*ite
kha	as *kh* in Ec*kh*art
ga	as *g* in *g*oat
gha	as *gh* in di*gh*ard
ṅ	as *n* in fi*n*ger
cha	as *ch* in *ch*anel
chha	as *chh* in staun*chh*eart
ja	as *j* in *j*ar
jha	as *dgeh* in he*dgeh*og
ñ	as *n* in lu*n*ch
ṭa	as *t* in *t*ub
ṭha	as *th* in ho*th*ead
ḍa	as *d* in *d*ivine
ḍha	as *dh* in re*dh*ead
ṇa	as *n* in bur*n*t
ta	as *t* in French word ma*t*ron
tha	as *th* in e*th*er
da	as *th* in ei*th*er
dha	as *dh* in Bud*dh*a
na	as *n* in *n*o
pa	as *p* in *p*ink
pha	as *ph* in u*ph*ill

ba	as *b* in *b*oy
bha	as *bh* in a*bh*or
ma	as *m* in *m*an
ya	as *y* in *y*es
ra	as *r* in *r*emember
la	as *l* in *l*ight
va	as *v* in *v*ine, as *w* in s*w*an
śha	as *sh* in *sh*ape
sa	as *s* in *s*in
ṣha	as *sh* in *sh*ow
ha	as *h* in *h*ut
kṣha	as *ksh* in frea*ksh*ow
jña	as *gy* in big*y*oung

ṛa   There is no sign in English to represent the sound ड़. It has been written as *ṛa* but the tip of the tongue quickly flaps down.

ṛha   There is no sign in English to represent the sound ढ़. It has been written as *ṛha* but the tip of the tongue quickly flaps down.

ṛī   *as ree in* spree

GLOSSARY

abhyās	practice
apauruṣheya	not created by any human
Brahman	another expression for God
bhakti	devotion
chintan	repetition of a thought, idea, or piece of knowledge, in the mind and intellect
devata	celestial god such as Indra, Agni (fire god), Vayu (wind god), etc
dharmaśālā	free hotel for travellers
guṇas	the three modes of material nature
guṇātīt	transcendental to the three modes of material nature
iṣhṭa dev	chosen form of God that one worships
karma	physical or mental actions performed by a person
karm yog	as explained in the Bhagavad Gita, the practice of keeping the mind attached to the Divine at all times while performing our everyday tasks
kriyamāṇ karma	the actions we perform in the present life of our free will

maya	God's material energy
mūrti	deity that is worshipped as a representation of God
paras	the mythical philosopher's stone
parikramā	circumambulation of a sacred object as a form of worship
prārabdh karma	the destiny one is allotted at the time of birth based on past karmas
prayojak kartā	one who bestows the power to perform actions, i.e. God
prayojya kartā	one who uses the power granted by the prayojak kartā, i.e. the individual soul
preya	opposite of śhreya; happiness which is like nectar in the beginning but transforms into poison later
puruṣhārth	actions performed by exercising one's freedom of choice
rājasic	of the mode of passion; one of the three modes of material nature
sādhaks	spiritual aspirants
sadhana	devotional practice
sañchit karma	a person's accumulated karmas of endless lifetimes
sattvic	of the mode of goodness; one of the three modes of material nature
śhāstras	scriptures
śhreya	happiness that seems like bitter poison in the beginning but becomes like sweet nectar later

śhruti	knowledge received through the oral tradition; it is used as another name for the Vedas
tāmasic	of the mode of ignorance; one of the three modes of material nature
tapasyā	voluntary privation; austerities
Vipassanā	a Buddhist technique involving concentration on the sensations of the body and the breath
vivek	power of discernment such that the intellect rules the mind

Let's Connect

If you enjoyed reading this book and would like to connect with Swami Mukundananda, you can reach him through any of the following channels:

Websites: www.jkyog.org, www.jkyog.in, www.7mindsetsforsuccess.org

YouTube Channels: 'Swami Mukundananda' and 'Swami Mukundananda Hindi'

Facebook: 'Swami Mukundananda' and 'Swami Mukundananda Hindi'

Instagram: 'Swami Mukundananda' and 'Swami Mukundananda Hindi'

LinkedIn: Swami Mukundananda

Podcasts: Apple, Google, SoundCloud, Spotify, Stitcher

JKYog Radio: TuneIn Radio app for iOS (Apple App Store) and Android (Google Play Store)

JKYog App: Available for iOS (Apple App Store) and Android (Google Play Store)

WhatsApp Daily Inspiration: We have two broadcast lists. You are welcome to join either or both.

USA: +1-512-808-6332

India: +91 84489 41008

Email: deskofswamiji@jkyog.org

To bring *7 Mindsets for Success, Happiness and Fulfilment* or Swami Mukundananda to your organisation—as Google, Verizon, Intel, Oracle, United Nations, Stanford University, Yale University, IITs and IIMs have—please write to deskofswamiji@jkyog.org.

Other Books by the Author

Art of Mind Management

Bhagavad Gita, The Song of God

Essence of Hinduism

Science of Healthy Diet

Spiritual Dialectics

Yoga for Mind, Body, and Soul

Books for Children

Bal-Mukund Wisdom Book

Festivals of India

Healthy Body, Healthy Mind: Yoga for Children

Inspiring Stories for Children (set of 4 books)

Mahabharat

My Best Friend Krishna

Ramayan

Saints of India

Made in the USA
San Bernardino,
CA